Into Africa

INTO AFRICA

*A True Story of
God's Faithfulness in a
Dry and Needy Land*

Winifred Green
with
Gayle Roper

Horizon Books
Camp Hill, Pennsylvania

DEDICATION

With gratitude and love
to my mother, GRACE HUFF,
who faithfully corresponded with us
through the years,
who kept the supply lines open
and who saved my letters
so this book could be written.

For Current Information on the Persecuted
Church, Please Contact:
The Voice of the Martyrs, Inc.
PO Box 443
Bartlesville, OK 74003
(918) 337-8015

Horizon Books
3825 Hartzdale Drive
Camp Hill, Pennsylvania 17011

Faithful, biblical publishing since 1883

ISBN: 0-88965-126-4
© 1995 by Horizon Books
All rights reserved
Printed in the United States of America

95 96 97 98 99 5 4 3 2 1

*Pronounciation key
for African names:*

A   as in father
E   as in pet
I   as in feet
O   as in pole
U   as in blue
R   is rolled

Contents

CHAPTER 1

Trouble in Torit

The drums began at 4 in the morning. *How strange,* I thought. *There's no reason, no obvious reason.* Here in Equatoria Province, Sudan, Africa, in 1955, the Latukas beat their drums for dances, for deaths and for a solid week before a hunting foray. Talk about hard on the nerves!

Of course someone could have died overnight but I didn't think so. The cadences of the drums were different from any I had heard before.

I lay under my mosquito netting, listening and wondering. Finally I got up, uneasy and on edge. I wished Dallas were here with me instead of on an overnight trip to the town of Juba with our four-year-old son Kennie.

"Why are the drums beating, Mom?" It was five-year-old Carolyn. I could only shake my head.

Kay, our towheaded; two-and-a-half-year-old, wakened, followed by her baby brother Carlie. I became caught up in the morning routine.

1

"Madame! Madame!" Our cook Yosefu burst into the house. "Bad things have happened in Torit! Men have been killed!"

My heart lurched. Dallas had to go through Torit on his way to and from Juba!

"Men from the north and men from the south are fighting!" Yosefu said.

Civil war, I thought. *The old hatreds have finally burst open.*

I waited impatiently for the daily radio transmissions of our Africa Inland Mission (AIM) missionaries in neighboring Congo. Every morning at 8 o'clock, the Congo stations checked in with each other. It was like listening in on a party line, and I loved it. We were so isolated here in Logotok that I reveled in the sound of American voices and the planning of everyday things like marketing excursions or transportation of kids to school and special things like weddings.

We had only a radio here in Logotok, so I couldn't participate in these discussions nor today could I ask any questions of anyone. But I could listen to hear if there was news.

There wasn't. I heard only general mission business until suddenly—and illegally—Sid Langford, one of our Sudan missionaries, cut into the transmission.

"Dallas, if you haven't left for Juba yet, don't go! If you haven't left for Juba yet, don't go! There's trouble in Torit and the roads are closed. Repeat. The roads are closed."

Don't go. Trouble in Torit.

"But Daddy's already gone," said Carolyn, her face uncertain. I nodded, trying to appear calm for her. "Shh. Listen."

"We'll try to get through to you to help you get Winifred and the kids to safety."

I was busy trying to reassure Carolyn and Kay that Daddy and Kennie were fine when Barbara Battye appeared at the door.

"*Hodi!*" she called.

"Come in," I said. "I just heard Sid on the radio. There's trouble in Torit."

Barb nodded. "I knew something was going on; I just didn't know what. The drums wakened me this morning, and on my way here, I saw the warriors streaming down the mountains with their spears and shields."

I picked up Carlie and gave him his bottle. He ate happily, the only one of us not concerned.

"We should pack," Barb said. "We need to be ready to evacuate. When's Dallas due back?"

"This morning between 10 and noon."

"We'll be ready when he gets here or when Sid gets here whoever arrives first."

I nodded, and we began packing the necessities for taking three little children—four when Kennie returned—across the mud track roads in the fierce African heat. We also locked up the dispensary, secured the store rooms, the best way we could secure mud huts

Barb was a good person to be with in a tough

3

time like this.

"You pronounce my name Batty," she said the first time we met her. "You can remember because I used to work in a mental hospital."

A single woman, she was very stable, gutsy and up to anything.

By 11:30 our van was loaded, but still no men had arrived. "I think we should leave," I said. "We'll meet the men on the road. But I can't drive."

"I haven't driven since I came to Africa," Barb said. "But you're right. We're too isolated here. We've got to leave. I'll just have to do the best I can. Too bad Dallas has the mission station's half-ton truck. I'd feel more secure in a truck with lower gears."

We loaded the kids into the van and started off. Yosefu came with us to help as needed. We had gone only three miles when we skidded on roads that were nothing but dust nine months of the year. This day they were slick from the rainy season.

The van came to rest up to its running board in mud. Our hearts still pounding, Barb and I climbed out to survey the damage.

"Looks like we're OK," I said. "Just stuck. Let me get Dallas' shovel. He never travels without it and a hoe and an ax."

But Dallas hadn't packed for this unexpected trip. I had. And I had forgotten the tools in my preoccupation with the kids and my missing husband. I couldn't believe that after two-and-a-half years on the field I was still such a novice.

"Don't worry," said the ever adaptable Barb. "We'll just use our hands."

After much digging and a few healthy pushes, we were back on the road with only a half hour lost.

My back, injured several years ago, told me quite clearly that it didn't approve of digging in mud and pushing cars. I gritted my teeth and tried to ignore the pain.

Unfortunately, on a road that was severely washboarded, the back pain couldn't be ignored. As we jounced and bounced, I fought to keep the slash of the muscle spasms from showing. Barb had enough to do in driving an unfamiliar vehicle on terrible roads and I didn't want the kids to worry.

We traveled three miles farther and came to a bad depression in the road. We got out of the car again and carried rocks to fill the declivity. The kids, Yosefu and I stood and watched while Barb tried out our construction. She got down the incline with no problem, but try as she would, she couldn't drive up the far side. She tried again and again, but the van insisted on stalling and sliding back.

"New plan," I said to Barb. "I just can't push anymore. Let me get behind the wheel. You and Yosefu can push. So can some of these Latukas who have come to watch us make fools of ourselves."

Everything we did fascinated and bewildered the Latukas, and they would often come from nowhere, like now, to stare. Undoubtedly they were thinking how much simpler things would be if we would only put everything on our heads, Carlie on my back and walk where we wanted to go.

Barb, Yosefu and some of the watchers took their places behind the van. I stomped hard on the gas pedal because I didn't know any better and with the mighty push from everyone, up and over the hill I went. We had again lost valuable time as we did at the next dip. And the next.

The most unnerving part of the trip was the passage of all this time and no Dallas and Kennie, no Sid.

Some 20 miles from Logotok we came to the first village actually on the road. Naked warriors all armed with spears lined both sides of the way.

We slowed, then stopped, uncertain how they would react to us. We had gotten along well with the Latukas through the years, but today was not a normal situation.

The warriors gathered around the van with scared expressions on their faces. When they recognized us, they broke into smiles of relief. The alleviation of tension was mutual and we greeted each other gladly.

"Madame," said one of the Latukas, "you should put a flag on your van so no one will hurt you. Others may not like you as much as we do. And wave your arm out the window. People won't kill you if they see your white arm."

We didn't have a flag, but as we continued on our way, we waved and waved. By now the road was lined with men carrying not only spears but rifles. They all looked scared and uncertain when they saw us, only to dissolve into smiles when they saw our white arms and recognized us.

I looked at the men and their spears with something like sympathy. They had no concept of the power and arms of the more modern northern troops. The Latukas were so unsophisticated that they couldn't begin to comprehend what would await them if civil war actually was about to begin.

"Madame," another group of soldiers told us, "you need a flag."

I pulled out one of Carlie's diapers and tied it to the van's spotlight, hoping the Africans were familiar with the white of the international peace flag.

Finally we reached Torit, a large town of several hundred, which was the site of a small southern military garrison and a small infirmary. There we found chaos and anarchy.

Trash littered the ground from the looting of shops and the stores that hadn't been looted were closed and barred. The streets were full of soldiers with rifles and machine guns, often aimed at us. Truckloads of soldiers patrolled the streets with no apparent plan for establishing authority. The most frightening thing to me was that so few wore uniforms. We couldn't tell if the men were southern troops whom we could expect to be friendly or northern troops who had no knowledge of us.

Rumors abounded about the people who had been killed. Northern Arabs who were residents of Torit had been burned to death in their houses. People had been buried alive. Babies had been cut up or bashed to death. Of course, the southerners said the northerners had fired the first shots and started it all.

We drove straight to Sid's house. I couldn't wait to be done with the tensions and terror of this trip. Only Sid wasn't there. The place was empty.

Barb and I looked at each other.

"Obviously we can't stay in Torit," she said. "It's too dangerous, especially with the kids. We can't go north to Juba because the ferry across the Nile isn't running anymore. We'll have to go south to Uganda. We'll be safer there."

I agreed. "Let's go to the district commissioner's and get the necessary papers for a border crossing."

We found the commissioner's office as deserted as Sid's home and we heard rumors that the commissioner himself had been killed.

"We've got to go whether we have papers or not," Barb said.

"Are you up to it?" I asked. "You've been driving for hours!"

"Have we a choice?"

As we drove south out of Torit, the road was thronged with refugees carrying all their belongings on their heads. The only difference between us and them was that we traveled more quickly—at least most of the time. We got stuck four more times and got ourselves out. Each time Carolyn stood by the roadside holding Carlie, Kay pressed close to her side.

"You kids are wonderful," I told them again and again. And they were. They didn't once complain or cry. They sat quietly in the backseat or stood solemnly by the side of the road, watching, listening, never demanding.

Once during a bad skid we slammed into a bank. A suitcase flew forward from the back and hit me in the head. The headache was just one more discomfort, arguing with my back over which would hurt more.

A truckload of soldiers stopped and pulled us free of the bank.

"Madame," they told us, keeping the rumor mill grinding well, "a northerner and his family have been killed here. They were locked in a grass hut, and it was set on fire."

I shivered. *If we hadn't had so many car problems, might we have been here when that happened? If it happened.*

It was fully dark when, back on the road, we saw another vehicle approaching. Barb blinked her lights. The approaching vehicle did the same, then fixed a spotlight on us. We slowed and saw a truck full of soldiers, all with guns pointed at us.

"The signal!" yelled their leader. "What is the signal?"

Dear Lord, I thought, *how did a quiet little girl from suburban Washington, D.C. ever get in the middle of a mess like this?*

CHAPTER 2

Days of Preparation

I was born on September 6, 1928, so I grew up in the Washington, D.C. area during the Great Depression and World War II. However, it was the upheavals in my personal life that mattered more to me than these national troubles.

The first large disruption occurred when I was four years old. Mom was going to have a new baby, and my father drove her to the hospital, dropped her at the front door and disappeared. Just like that. To the best of my knowledge I never saw him again and neither did Mom. He certainly never saw his second daughter, my new sister, Thelma.

We moved in with my grandparents, after my father left and Mom took a succession of small jobs to feed us. I remember times of crying with fear when she would leave me. What if she never came back either? But she returned each day, tired but completely faithful to Thelma and me.

Grandma took on the raising of us girls, a considerable job in the best of circumstances, a monumental undertaking when Thelma became ill at 18 months of age.

"She's very sick, honey," Grandma told me. "And she'll become sicker and sicker."

And she did, the second major disruption in my life. Soon Grandma spent almost all day holding Thelma as she became blind and increasingly spastic. Eventually she could neither stand, sit, hear nor speak. Ovaltine was the only nourishment she could take. I was eight when Thelma died at four.

The next major change occurred when I was 10 and Mom met Jack Huff, a career soldier who was a kind and thoughtful man. They met at a night school bookkeeping course I remember them studying together in Grandma and Grandpa's living room.

When they married, we moved to a third floor apartment. The feel of our home became pleasant and light and Mom, who kept on working, was genuinely happy.

I wasn't. I didn't like myself or my life and my thoughts were melancholy and full of self-loathing. I didn't have many friends and not having a "real" father made me different. When Mom became Grace Huff, I remained Winifred Gordon, making me feel my difference all the more keenly.

One genuinely joyous day in my life was the birth of my sister Jackie when I was 12. I couldn't imagine a more wonderful thing happening to me. I loved her little fingers and toes and holding her was my great delight. I considered myself her second mother and I enjoyed taking care of her.

We had moved, just before Jackie's birth, into the house two doors from Grandma and Grandpa. Since I considered Grandma one of the world's great cooks, I thoroughly approved of this move because it meant I could eat at her house frequently.

My stepfather, Jack, was a mess sergeant assigned to Army Headquarters in Washington.

"Come on, Winifred," he said one Memorial Day. "We'll let Mom and Jackie stay here while we go to the biggest picnic you'll ever see."

Off we went to Arlington National Cemetery where Jack's assignment was to feed all the military men involved in the remembrance ceremonies.

"Here's your dinner," he said, sitting me down with a huge sandwich just like the ones he was feeding the soldiers. I looked at it, then at Jack and the soldiers. To everyone's delight I devoured the whole thing just like the men.

I was 13 when I was invited to go to a youth meeting. I was shocked at how different this meeting was from what I was used to. I'd gone to church regularly because Mom and Grandma and Grandpa were charter members of our church, but I had never seen or heard anything like this meeting.

"Let me tell you what God's been doing in my life," said one young person.

"I read this verse this week and it was a wonderful promise to me," said another.

"I became a Christian when I finally realized that I was a sinner and needed God," said a third.

Then most of the young people prayed aloud.

I was very aware that I couldn't tell about anything God was doing for me, nor could I pray aloud if I were asked to. I didn't like the feeling of being unprepared.

I'll just write a prayer and a testimony before the next meeting, I thought. *Then I'll memorize it and know what to say. That way I'll sound just like them.*

I felt it very important not to look foolish if I could so easily avoid it.

Somehow I never got around to writing a thing either that week or the next. I just held my breath and tried to look like I was as confident as everyone else.

At the third meeting a young man named Brandt Reed was the special speaker. His enthusiasm for God touched me.

"It isn't enough to be aware of God and Jesus, you know," he said. "You must believe all on your own that you are lost and that Jesus died to save you. You must accept Jesus as your Savior."

That night I believed and committed my life to God.

God provided a wonderful help for me in those days. Myrtle Schwartz, a young married woman, took an interest in me. Many afternoons after school I walked several miles to her home to talk with her as she ironed or did housework.

"I don't understand *how* I consecrate myself to God, Myrtie," I said. "And why would God want me?"

"God wants you because He loves you," Myrtie told me. "And consecrating yourself to God means living for Him, making decisions that please Him. It means being pure and holy."

"The Bible says I'm to consecrate my members. How do I do that?"

"Your members are your hands and feet and your mouth and mind," Myrtie said. "Commit them to God and His service."

Oh, Lord, I'd think, *make me the Christian You want me to be.*

I had purpose in my life now and the feelings of self-loathing lessened as my knowledge of God grew. If He loved me, I must be OK or He could make me OK. Joy in God and who He was became the cornerstone of my life.

To occupy myself all those long, lonely afternoons after school when I was the only one in our house, I taught myself to play hymns on the piano. I knew where middle C was, so I counted up the lines and spaces of the music, then up the keys, to find what note I should play. I learned the melody first. Then I'd add the alto notes. Months later I'd add the bass clef.

I was 14 when I first heard a missionary speaker and I was totally taken with his message. He talked about people in South America who had never before heard the name of Jesus.

People who didn't even know there was a Jesus? I couldn't believe it. *Those poor people!*

When the speaker asked, "Who is willing to serve God on the mission field?", I knew I was.

After the meeting I approached the man. "I want to be a missionary," I said. "I'm willing to stop school next week and go wherever you tell me."

With great kindness and not a hint of a smile, he said, "I'm sure God has great things for you, but I think He can use you best if you complete your education. Don't rush Him."

The logic of his answer made sense to me, and I was satisfied to wait a few years before I sailed off to some unknown part of the earth as God's ambassador.

During these mid-teen years, I determined that I needed to be baptized as a believer. I selected a Baptist church in our neighborhood for the wonderful occasion. The day of a baptismal service, I sneaked out of the house with my towel and sheet and hurried to the church. I met with the deacons and gave my testimony as clearly as I could despite my nervousness.

"Wonderful," the men said, smiling. "We

have just one question for you. You will be joining our church, won't you?"

I was appalled. "Oh, no," I said. "My parents would never allow it."

"Then we're sorry," they said. "We can't baptize you."

I was devastated. I had never imagined such a thing. It took me some time to recover from the hurt. A year or so later, with great joy, I was baptized by immersion at a summer camp.

Through my high school years I continued my close friendship with Myrtie, and I became more and more involved in Christian service. Those lonely afternoons at the piano proved providential as I played for youth meetings. I became part of a girls' group called the Hi-Light Trio. We sang in churches all over the Washington area—and I discovered many good churches.

I graduated from 12th grade at 16 and applied for nurse's training. Ever since I had gone to the hospital with my mother to visit my great-grandmother when I was a child, I had wanted to be a nurse. I had watched those gentle, caring women with fascination as they helped Grandma Jo and I wanted to become just such a woman.

"I regret to inform you that you are too young to attend nursing school," I was told.

"But I graduated and did very well academically!" I protested.

"No matter. You're too young. Rules, you know."

What a blow. So I passed the year until I was 17 by taking college courses until I was permitted to begin what I considered to be the schooling that counted.

Finances have been a major consideration all my life and were very much an issue in terms of my post high school education.

Dear Lord, I'd pray, *where will the money for nursing school come from?*

During World War II, the Nurse Cadet Program was developed to supply the vast numbers of nurses needed by the armed forces. All costs of nursing education were covered by Uncle Sam in return for service. I applied to be part of the program through Garfield Hospital in Washington, D.C. and was accepted to begin training in September 1945. Though the war ended in August 1945, the commitments to all those previously accepted into the program were honored. My nursing education was paid in full by the government though the war's end removed my obligation to be in the service.

I loved nurse's training from the beginning. It was all that I had hoped, even down to the white stockings and starched blue and white striped dress of my student uniform. The coveted white uniform of a registered nurse was a goal I felt worth pursuing. Three hard situations occurred that challenged my ability to reach that goal.

First, Jack Huff died unexpectedly as the result of abdominal surgery. Mom was devastated, and

I shared her grief. He had been kind to me, and I knew I would miss him.

By now Mom worked for my grandfather, a civil engineer. He had trained her, and she served as his Girl Friday. The two of them would leave at 6 in the morning and return at 6 in the evening. Grandma raised Jackie as she had raised me.

In my second year of training, we learned that my real father had committed suicide. For some reason, I was invited to his viewing. I was a very nervous 18-year-old when I finally met the half of my family I had never known. It was with great surprise that I discovered that they were Christians.

I was involved in the psychiatric part of my studies, temporarily affiliated with the local psychiatric facility at St. Elizabeth's Hospital, when my father died. I immediately saw in myself all the symptoms exhibited by patients in my care. I went to my supervisor, greatly concerned about my stability, wondering if his depression would be inherited by me.

"Don't worry, Miss Gordon. There's nothing wrong with you. You're feeling exactly as you should after such an experience and you're working through your feelings. Your patients never get beyond the feeling part."

If I was fine, I knew it was because of the Lord and His power in my life. Where would I be without His balance and strength?

The third major trauma of my training years

was physical. I injured my back seriously and with debilitating effect. How I hurt myself I don't know. I assume it was in handling a patient. What I do know is that pain became a regular feature of my life, and I missed many days of classes and ward work.

To counter these difficult things, at the same time, God gave me the blessing of a lifetime. I met Dallas Green.

CHAPTER 3

Falling in Love

Would you like some more cocoa?" I asked, offering my pitcher to people as I walked through the crowd at Grace Baptist Church one Sunday night. In those early post-war days, young men and women home from various points of the world filled churches and young adult programs.

"I'd like some," said a young man, sticking his empty cup out before him.

I peered into my pitcher. Enough for one more. I poured.

"Thanks," he said. "You're Winifred Gordon, aren't you?"

I looked at him and nodded. I was certain I'd never met him before, but that wasn't surprising. Grace Baptist wasn't my usual church. I was attending now because I was in my psychiatric affiliation at nearby St. Elizabeth's Hospital.

"I'm Dallas Green," he said. "I know who you are because I was here the night you sang

21

and gave your testimony about six months ago."

I nodded, pleased this nice looking guy re-membered me.

"You're going to be a nurse, right?" he asked.

"I'm at St. E's right now," I said.

"I bet I know your phone number," he said and rattled off my hall number.

"How do you know that?" I asked.

He grinned. He had a very delightful, very warm smile.

"I've been in telephone communications for the last few years," he said. "I know such things."

"And I'm supposed to believe this?"

He shrugged. "Of course."

"Come on," I said. "Tell me. How do you know the number?"

He grinned again. "I used to date another nurse at St. E's."

I nodded, smiling back. "I should have known." I started for the kitchen and another pitcherful of cocoa.

"Not so fast," Dallas said. "I wanted to ask if I could take you home tonight."

When the evening broke up, I found Dallas at my elbow.

"Come on," he said.

He led me outside and walked me to the bus stop. When the bus came, he ushered me on board like it was our private car.

"Where do you come from?" I asked. "Your

accent isn't exactly typical Washington."

"Ahoskie, North Carolina," he said, pronouncing the state like there were no *R*s in its name. "Up in the northeast corner near nowhere."

I learned he had been in the service for four years, more specifically in the Signal Corps, 8th Air Force, stationed in Europe for three years in telephone communications. He had returned to civilian ranks in August, 1945, three months after VE Day.

"If you're from North Carolina," I said, "what are you doing in Washington?"

"I'm at George Washington University studying civil engineering."

"GI Bill?" I asked.

"Absolutely," he said.

"And your family?"

"I'm the oldest of three," he said. "I've a brother and sister."

"How about your family?"

I told him about Mom and Jackie and my grandparents and the death of my stepfather. I liked his immediate show of interest and concern for the events big and small in my life.

"I've found that the Lord helps me when hard things hit," I said. "Don't you?"

"Unfortunately the war years were not good years for me spiritually," he said. "I'm from a Christian family but I got very far from God. It's just recently that the Lord has been working in my life and I'm finally getting back to where I should be."

I was afraid that when my rotation at St. E's ended, so would Dallas' interest in me. A 20-minute bus ride to the hospital wasn't too bad, especially since he lived just down the street from St. E's. What about when I did pediatrics across town and the ride was 45 minutes? Or when I returned to Garfield and the ride was 45 minutes plus a transfer to a trolley and 20 more minutes? How many men would be willing to undergo that tedium just to talk to me?

To my surprise and delight, Dallas was willing, even eager, in spite of the many nights when the bus had stopped running by the time of his return trip and he had to walk all the way home.

Amazing, I thought. *If he's willing to travel these distances, maybe we have something here.*

We had been dating about six months when he told me he was seriously thinking of leaving George Washington.

"What for?" I asked. "You're doing so well."

"The Lord is working in my heart, and I think He's calling me into fulltime service of some kind."

"That's wonderful!" I said, thrilled. "Absolutely wonderful."

"I think I'll transfer to Providence Bible College," he said. "I'll get my education in Bible there and be ready for whatever the Lord wants."

"Providence as in Rhode Island?" So far

away. No bus rides home from there.

I'd discovered slowly over the months that buses were the high point of spending for Dallas. Any money he had went to supporting his family. When his father retired for the second time at the War's end, he was in his late 60s and unable to find a good job. Dallas contributed all he could to the family coffers and provided their housing from his GI Bill.

We had been dating for nine months when Dallas asked me to marry him. I was more than willing to say yes. I might spend my married life traveling by bus, but I'd be happy with this considerate and committed man.

Five months after we became engaged, I waved goodbye as Dallas set off in September, 1948, for Providence, Rhode Island. By bus. With everything he owned in one suitcase. Plans were for us to marry in December, four very long months away. Providence Bible College rules forbad first year students marrying, but rules were frequently relaxed for returning vets and we looked forward to our wedding.

"As soon as you find us a place to live," I wrote, "tell me all about it. I want to know how many rooms and what color the walls are and everything. And what color's the bathroom so I can get towels to match?"

Letter after letter arrived from Providence, including the one that told me Dallas had finally found an apartment for us. None of the letters told me anything about this marvelous find in a day of very tight housing.

While I waited for the months to pass, I finished my nurse's training. My class had been graduated in September, 1948, and I had been allowed to take part in the ceremony with them, but I wasn't given my diploma or permitted to wear my white uniform yet. I had too much floor time to make up because of days lost to pain from my back injury. Hospital rules required that I make up every day I had missed. I finally became an official graduate of Garfield Hospital with my diploma dated December 28, 1948, though I'd actually finished my work a few days before.

On December 28, 1948, I also became Mrs. Dallas Green.

During those lonely months Dallas was in Providence, I had planned our wedding down to the minutest detail. My bridesmaids wore dark red velvet and I wore a white satin gown Grandma made for me. Dallas was so handsome, and I enjoyed every minute of my lovely day.

For the first night of our honeymoon, a friend took us to a nearby hotel. The next day Dallas' Aunt Maggie Sue drove us to Richmond, Virginia, playing country-western music full volume the whole way. We spent two nights in her spare bedroom. Her two teenage sons were fascinated with our visit and its reason. For me it was all very embarrassing being there.

We returned by train to Mom's for a night, then were to join a teacher from PBC and drive to Providence with her and her daughter. Instead we received a call.

"I'm feeling so sick," the teacher said. "I can't face the drive to Providence. My daughter and I are taking the train home. Would you mind driving my car for me, Dallas?"

We drove from Washington to Providence with as many of our wedding gifts as we could stuff in the car. Finally we pulled up in front of a former nursing home that had been converted into apartments. Our home.

"Come on," Dallas said, taking my hand.

He led me up two flights of stairs and down a long hall to the back of the building.

"This is it," he said as he threw open the door.

"You've got to carry me over the threshold," I said.

Gallantly he lifted me and carried me into our first home, an L-shaped, battleship gray room. An icebox sat just inside the front door on the left and a sink was against the facing wall beside a two burner hot plate. Around the bend in the L was a sofa bed and an armoire. When the bed was open, we had to climb over it to get to the clothes in the armoire.

"The whole apartment's no bigger than a closet!" I said.

Dallas nodded, pleased at how perceptive I was. "It used to be a linen closet when this was a nursing home."

"Well, that explains that," I said. "Now I don't mean to complain, but that—" I pointed. "That is not a refrigerator. It's an icebox."

"The ice man will bring the ice up for you," Dallas assured me.

I looked around. "Where's the bathroom?"

"Down the hall and around the corner," he said. "We don't have to share it with too many people."

"No wonder you wouldn't write me anything about the place," I said. Buses began to look roomy and comfortable.

Somehow, in the middle of all this chaos and confusion and joy, I became pregnant right away and Carolyn Ruth was born on September 29, 1949. By then we had moved down one floor to an apartment with two bedrooms and a bath. On April 21, 1951, Kenneth Douglas joined the family.

During this time, several strands came together for Dallas that confirmed in his heart a call to missions, specifically to the Sudan in Africa.

One influence was another student at PBC named Alice Wentworth, an African young woman and the adopted daughter of missionaries. We listened to her stories of home with fascination.

We also met Olive Love, a veteran missionary to the Congo who spoke at our church while on furlough. Again her stories drew us in an unusual way.

At the same time Dallas heard much about Africa Inland Mission because the college president and one of the professors were AIM board members who had just returned from a trip to the field.

One specific day the scheduled chapel speaker became ill. Replacing him was the director of Africa Inland Mission who had just returned from the same field visit. Much of what he spoke about was the new field of the Sudan, a pioneer venture just opening up.

His stories fired Dallas' imagination. He came home and announced, "That's what we're going to do, honey. We're going to go to the Sudan."

I nodded. "Sounds fine to me."

"Are you serious?" he asked. Apparently he didn't expect me to agree so easily.

I nodded. "You know I've always felt inclined toward missions."

"But this is pioneer work, hard work, in-the-middle-of-nowhere work."

I nodded again. "Sounds fine to me."

"What confirmation!" His eyes were alight as he grabbed me and hugged me.

I was finally going to be a missionary after all.

CHAPTER 4

Flying Off into the Unknown

I didn't sleep at all the night before we left for Sudan. Besides being anxious, I kept reviewing my list of things to do. What had I forgotten?

Dear God, help me remember everything the kids will need. I might not be able to get it for four years if I forget it.

"Bring five sizes of shoes for the children to grow into," we had been told. "Especially if they are hard on shoes."

Five pair per child? We now had a third baby, Marilyn Kay, born October 20, 1952. How did I know if my three-month-old Kay would grow up to be hard on shoes? Besides, where would we get the money for five pair per child? We could barely afford the requisite pair for present use.

"Everyone gets malaria," we were told. "Bring thousands of malarial prophylactics.

And there are lots of creeping things under the mike."

Germs under the microscope, I finally translated. We loaded up on malaria medicine and other medical supplies from adhesive bandages and cough medicine to antiseptics and aspirin, from penicillin and sulfa to deodorant and toothpaste. We bought large quantities of baby lotion, baby powder and face soap.

"Why don't we just live like the Africans?" we asked, thinking how it would simplify things.

"No," came the reply. "You wouldn't be happy in their type home or with their food. Since we don't look like them, they expect us to be different. Besides, our conveniences are what give us time for the work we're here to do."

"I guess that makes sense," I said to Dallas. "I just wish we knew more!"

"Get a heavy truck as your vehicle," we were told. "The roads are devastating to anything lighter. Uncle John Buyse just ruined his truck. Again."

"No, no," said others. "You have a family to consider. Bring a sturdy car that will allow you to transport them. You can always borrow a truck if you need to haul heavy things."

All advisors were agreed that we should bring lots of spare parts for whatever vehicle we purchased. "You know, whatever goes with the ordinary wear of a car for four years."

We knew that the ordinary wear of a car in America and the ordinary wear of a car in Sudan were vastly different, and we hadn't the vaguest idea what we would need.

God finally settled the issue by wonderfully providing a 1951 Chevrolet Carry-All, or van, and lots of spare parts. We shipped the Carry-All and the bulk of our large supplies including a desk, mattresses, an ironing board and a kitchen table and chairs. We also purchased or were given sheets, towels, mosquito netting, flashlights, sun helmets and a multitude of other things which we stuffed in our suitcases.

Since Dallas had graduated from PBC, he had been serving as interim pastor at the First Baptist Church in Long Branch, New Jersey. The interim status was perfect for our travels to raise support. Many of the churches that pledged to help us with prayer and finances were churches Dallas had preached in as a student at PBC. The Long Branch church was also firmly and enthusiastically supportive.

Suddenly only the last minute things remained to be done. We added Kay's picture to my passport and got yellow fever shots. We crammed the suitcases until we were afraid they would burst.

The temperature in New York City was 10 degrees the Monday we left. We wrapped Kay in four blankets, took Carolyn and Kennie by the hand and collected Kay's baby paraphernalia. Dallas was wearing the two pairs of pants, shirt, sweater, jacket, suitcoat and overcoat the suitcases simply refused to accommodate.

Family and friends escorted us, Dallas waddling slightly, to Idlewilde Airport and saw us aboard our propeller driven TWA Constellation. Our baggage was 18 pounds overweight, no surprise, but we weren't charged for it. We paid the $12 extra that would provide all of us with all our meals on the planes for the length of our air journey. We were saving $500 traveling tourist rate and had expected to have to buy our meals at stopovers. How gracious God's provision was for us as we started on our great advernture.

At 3 o'clock on the afternoon of January 26, 1953, Dallas and I and the kids took off for Sudan, Africa. If we had forgotten anything, it was too late now. With a feeling of unreality, we ate our fried chicken dinner somewhere over the Atlantic. We were finally on our way to become part of a pioneer work about which we knew surprisingly little. We just *knew* God had called us.

Of course we were aware of encyclopedia facts about Sudan:

It is the largest country in Africa, as large as the United States east of the Mississippi.

It is between Egypt on the north and Uganda on the south, Ethiopia on the east and Chad on the west.

It had been a protectorate of Egypt and Great Britain since 1899 and was officially called the Anglo-Egyptian Sudan.

The Nile River system runs through the country, the White Nile coming up from the south to meet the Blue Nile, coming—from the east. They met at Khartoum, the nation's capital.

The people of the northern two-thirds of the country were largely Arabs and Moslems.

The people of the southern third of the country were blacks and pagans.

The north and south were separated topographically by the Sudd area, one of the largest marshes in the world.

The people of the north and south disliked and distrusted each other intensely.

Then there was the very brief history of missions in Sudan, "land of the blacks." In September 1949, John and Mabel Buyse, both 66 years old and veteran missionaries to Uganda and Bill and Dorothy Beatty and their young son Barry became AIM's first representatives in southern Sudan. Over the next three years, four single women and a doctor and his wife joined the AIM team.

These 10 people were spread among three stations with magical names like Opari and Katire Ayom and Logotok, the newest and most remote. Our assignment was to join Dr. Doug and Kim Reitsma, Barbara Battye and Martha Hughell at Logotok among the Latuka people.

"The work is absolutely primitive, starting from scratch," we were told. "There are about

90,000 Latukas who are a fine upstanding cattle people. Water here in southern Sudan is always problematic, located as the area is near the equator. However, there is a well with an abundant supply of water in Logotok."

On we flew to Shannon, Ireland (refuel); London, England (layover); Nice, France (refuel); Malta (layover); Benini, Libya (refuel); Wadi Halfa, Sudan (layover); and finally to Juba, Sudan.

On the London layover we had spent our first night as a family in a hotel. Our room had three single beds and a crib, so Kay slept in a dresser drawer. We had a small electric heater, but nothing we could do made it produce any heat.

Finally a chambermaid came by.

"We can't get any heat out of this heater," we told her.

"Well, blimey," she said, looking at us in kindly disbelief. "Ye have t' put a shilling in it."

Through the night we put shilling after shilling after shilling into the thing, but it remained so cold that we slept huddled in two beds with all our clothes on under all the available blankets. Still, we shivered the night away.

We left London the day we were scheduled to arrive in Juba. Lesson number one in the uncertainties of world travel.

When we landed at Malta, we followed our standard family formation. I carried Kay and the diaper bag and held two harnesses that were around Carolyn and Kennie. Dallas carried a two-gallon thermos of boiled water, a TWA bag of kid supplies and took care of customs and passports. Often he was reduced to carrying the papers in his teeth.

We had barely taken off from Malta when one of our plane's engines suddenly died. I stared nervously at the unmoving propeller as we limped slowly back to the airport. The side benefit of this harrowing experience was the chance to enjoy an extra day on this lovely island while another engine was flown in from England.

Our last layover was in Wadi Halfa, just south of the Egyptian-Sudan border.

"But we're so close," I said.

"Air-Work does not fly at night, Madame," I was told.

The next morning Dallas left our room to see about getting some boiled water for Kay's formula. We carried powdered Klim (milk spelled backwards) with us to mix with the water in a bottle as Kay needed it.

I was dressing when I heard someone in the room.

"That was fast," I said, turning around.

It wasn't Dallas. A turbaned, white gowned figure was in the room, returning Kay's baby bottles we had sent to be boiled. He had each of the fingers of one hand in a bottle and held the nipples in his other large, unsanitary palm. Lesson number one in the lack of respect for privacy in that part of the world. Lesson number one in the lack of sanitation.

Sunday morning, a full week after we left New York, we finally left for Juba on the last leg of the air journey. I changed the kids' clothes on the plane, putting new nylon dresses on Carolyn and Kay and new long pants on Kennie. I wanted us to make a good impression.

We flew low. The terrain was wasteland as far as I could see.

"What will be the temperature?" I asked the attendant.

"I don't know," she said. "This is my first trip to Juba."

Mine, too, I thought as we circled the grass hut that turned out to be the Juba Airport.

We had arrived.

CHAPTER 5

Shocking Arrival in Sudan

"Mom, Dad." Carolyn looked eagerly around the Juba Airport, a large grass roof that shaded several wooden benches and the customs table. "Where are all the boys and girls? I want to tell them about Jesus."

"We'll meet them later," I said, trying to get my breath in the absolutely staggering heat. "Be patient, sweetheart."

"OK." She was satisfied.

We watched our plane take off, heading for the bustling city of Nairobi, Kenya. Our 14 traveling companions, with us since Malta, had bid us farewell with pity and great concern on their faces and in their voices.

I was concerned myself as we stood, dressed in our Sunday best with our winter coats over our arms. I wondered if we looked as foolish as I felt.

"Where's Uncle John?" I said.

Dallas shook his head. "Let me see about getting us into town."

Soon we were bouncing over a dirt road in the back of an open-bed truck.

"I'm hot," said Kennie.

"Me, too," said Carolyn.

"Me, too," said Dallas.

"A week ago we were in New York where it was 10 degrees." I fanned myself with a piece of tissue, the only thing readily at hand. "What do you think it is here?"

"Easily 100." Dallas wiped his streaming forehead on his sleeve. "Probably more."

Kennie lay his head in my lap, tired in spite of sleeping on the plane all morning. I brushed my hand across his forehead. Startled, I realized Kennie was more than just hot and tired. He was feverish. As soon as we reached Juba and the hotel, I took his temperature. 105!

Fortunately we found Uncle John Buyse was waiting for us.

"I've been here since Thursday," he said cheerfully.

"We got held up in London and Malta," we explained, all apologies. "We didn't know how to reach you."

"Don't worry about it," he said, obviously not the least bit concerned. "I know there was no way to contact me. Out here you just learn to be flexible and get used to waiting."

We let Kennie rest until evening, but his temperature remained elevated. We found an

Egyptian doctor in our hotel, but he had no medicine with him. It was Monday morning before we were finally able to get Kennie a shot of penicillin. Then his temperature fell quickly to 101.

Lord, learning flexibility and waiting while one of my kids is involved is hard! You're going to have to help me.

Monday Uncle John took us shopping for necessities to take with us to Logotok. We wouldn't be back to the suks or stores for two or three months because we would have no transportation until our Carry-All arrived. Overwhelmed by the strangeness of everything, we depended heavily on Uncle John.

"Get 100 pounds of flour," he said. "Fifty pounds of sugar. Ten pounds of butter and canned cheese. Five cans of dried oatmeal. Lots and lots of canned soup."

Canned cheese. Canned oatmeal. I'd never seen these products packaged that way before, though I could see that with the extreme heat, it was a superb way to handle them.

I could also see that learning to shop in Africa would be very intimidating and frightening. My circumscribed American life in Washington, Providence and Long Branch, New Jersey, did little to prepare me for the color, chaos and foreignness of the suks of Sudan. First, there was the money issue. Then I was used to shopping for small quantities and found buying such large amounts unnerving.

And everything was either totally new or packaged totally differently from what I was familiar with.

"Ox-tail soup?" I said uncertainly.

"You'll love it," Uncle John said. "Or at least you'll get used to it. We don't have much variety to change from here."

The suks, really nothing more than small grass shacks, sold everything from English canned soups, beads and felt hats to hoes, buckets and knives. Well-dressed Africans walked casually through the suks side by side with others wearing not one stitch of clothing. Most of the latter couldn't afford to buy anything but seemed to get great joy out of looking.

"I knew it was going to be different," I said to Dallas later that night, my mind whirling at all the new sights and smells and experiences. "But I didn't know it would be *this* different."

Tuesday morning we began the 125-mile trip to Logotok with all our luggage and supplies as well as all of Uncle John's purchases, including 300 pounds of cement, packed into his three-quarter-ton pickup. We three adults and the three children crammed into the cab, a child on both Dallas' and my laps and the third squashed between us. Uncle John's four African "boys" perched in back on top of the gear.

"Never go anywhere without boys," Uncle John said. "They are invaluable helps in so many ways."

Since Juba is on the west side of the Nile and Logotok is on the east we had to make a ferry crossing. When I saw the ferry, I was floored.

"It's only a raft!" I said.

"With pontoons for flotation," said Uncle John as if that were supposed to make me feel better.

Dallas and I huddled with the children on the bank as Uncle John drove the truck on board. As the ferry tilted under the weight, I wondered how many trucks had quietly slid into the river, taking their drivers and precious cargoes with them.

On the ferry with us were goats, cows, chickens, produce, men, women with their babies on their backs, children, large grass baskets and innumerable other things. The ferrymen poled the raft from one side of the river to the other. We Greens seemed the only ones concerned about the weight and distribution of the load and the stability of the craft.

It only took a few minutes on the road for us to appreciate the steadiness of the ferry. The road was a huge, horrendous washboard! The bumps were a foot high every three or four feet for 85 miles. It had not rained in four months, and dust was everywhere—in our hair, in our eyes, in our teeth, in our ears.

The truck shook and rattled and complained. We bumped our heads repeatedly on the roof and elbowed each other unintentionally. Every so often we managed to get a word from one side of the cab to the other by the man in the middle repeating it, but conversation was impossible because of the noise.

After a seemingly endless time we reached Torit where Uncle John had to see the district commissioner. While there we discovered that the center bolt on the rear spring of the truck had broken.

"We have to unload and replace it," said Uncle John so calmly that I got another insight into flexibility in Sudan. "If I can find another."

Providentially there was another bolt in Torit. We waited a hot, uncomfortable six hours in a grass hut, using our suitcases as chairs, while the truck was unloaded, repaired and reloaded.

About this time, Carolyn's temperature began rising, reaching toward Kennie's which had already gone back up. I was very worried because when it came to my kids, I was more the concerned mom than the trained nurse.

"There'll be medicine in Logotok," Uncle John assured me. "And I'll get you there as fast as I can. Don't worry."

Finally we were back on the road for the final 40 miles. It was a good thing no one said, "I'm hungry," because, in spite of all that flour back in the bed of the truck, there was no food to eat.

Fifteen miles from Logotok we turned off the main road Then we learned what "bad" really meant. We jounced and bumped over what was little more than a dirt track.

The worst were the dried up river beds. We went over about five of them, down 10 feet, across three feet, then up the other side, all the while going over two and three foot boulders, tree stumps and innumerable smaller rocks. It took us an hour and a half to go 15 miles.

"Just be glad it isn't rainy season," Uncle John said happily as I tried to find some saliva in my mouth but found only dust. "Then we wouldn't be able to get across these river beds at all. We'd just have to stay put on the side of the river where we happened to be until the water receded."

Wonderful, I thought. *But at least I'd be able to swallow.*

As we drove up the Logotok road, Uncle John beeped the horn for about a mile. One by one we saw three lights appear, the kerosene lanterns of Martha Hughell, Barbara Battye and Hank Senff. They and about 15 Latukas greeted us, a thoroughly weary and battered crew.

A two-cent postcard from AIM to my mother:

February 2, 1953:

A cable received this morning informed us that the Dallas Green family reached the Sudan safely yesterday. We know that you will rejoice with us that the Lord has brought them to their destination safely.

CHAPTER 6

Culture Shock at Logotok

Y ou'll be staying in Dr. Reitsma's house while he and Kim and their daughter Susie are on vacation in Congo," Uncle John said.

"What about our house?" we asked.

"Your house?" Uncle John looked confused.

"We were told there'd be a house for us when we got here," Dallas said.

Uncle John shook his head. "I'm sorry. It's just so hard to get any work done here at Logotok."

Dallas and I swallowed our disappointment and followed Barb and the others across the compound. As we walked in the door of Reitsmas' thatched roof hut, lantern held high, thousands of big red ants scurried everywhere. Though my stomach clutched, I was too tired to react further.

Some school boys dragged a large metal tub

into the house and filled it with hot water. We sponge bathed the whole family, removing a few layers of grime. Then we went to Barb and Martha's house for a late dinner.

"If it looks a little warmed over," Barb said, "it's because we expected you a few days ago."

"It was supposed to take us four days to get here," said Dallas. "Instead it took us nine."

After dinner we returned to the Reitsmas' house and went to bed. We tucked mosquito netting suspended from bamboo strips around the kids and ourselves and slept until the morning heat became unbearable.

I opened my eyes in the bright sunshine and screamed.

A fierce looking Latuka man wearing nothing was walking through the room!

"Easy, honey," said Dallas. "It's just a houseboy."

"Houseboy, my eye! He's a man! And he's naked! "

"Relax," Dallas said. "Look, He's here to get Doug's ax to chop wood for the stove out back."

I watched his retreating figure, my heart calming slowly. "Didn't he ever hear of knocking?"

No, it turned out. The Latukas hadn't heard of knocking. They had no sense of privacy and had to be taught not to walk in whenever they felt like it. That didn't stop them from peering in the windows to watch us.

We ate our meals for the first five days with Barb and Martha, a nurse with training in translation techniques from the Summer Institute of Linguistics. The women had just returned from Congo and had an abundance of carrots, beets, cabbage and cauliflower.

"How come," I asked Dallas one evening after dinner, "you never ate those vegetables back in the States?"

"I ate cabbage," he said like it had been a major accomplishment. "But I'm getting an idea how rare fresh vegetables are out here. I'd better eat them while I can even if I don't like them."

We didn't realize immediately how fortunate we were to have meat either. Hank, a veteran missionary from the Congo who had come to help with the pioneer efforts in Sudan, had shot a hartebeest and an antelope in honor of our coming. Often, though, long spans of time passed with no animals bagged. If there was nothing to shoot at, even Hank's famous, "Well, in Congo we did it this way . . ." had no effect.

The mission station at Logotok was situated on a plain, elevation 1,600 feet, with a horseshoe of mountains surrounding it. The horseshoe opened on the northeast, and the encircling hills rose 900 feet above the plain. Several tiny villages clung to these hills. Each village consisted of seven to 15 huts enclosed in a bamboo stockade intended to both contain the livestock and protect it and the villagers from wild animals. The huts had thick mud walls and high conical grass roofs with a space between the two of six to eight inches. This space let in not only air but also the insect and lizard world.

When we arrived at Logotok, it had not rained for over five months, and the ground and mountainside were devoid of any green except for an occasional tree. Fires raged on the mountains, a fearful thing to people who lived in thatched roof huts.

Every morning the women came down the mountains to gather wood, to find water and to work in their gardens.

"So what do the men do?" I asked Barb and Martha.

"Nothing," Martha said.

"That's not quite right," said Barb. "Once a year they get together and break ground for the gardens."

"True," agreed Martha. "And every so often they hunt."

"They don't see any need to work," Barb explained. "They don't need money. They eat only one meal a day, a thick porridge made of ground grain and they snack on raw peanuts. They don't wear clothes." She shrugged. "So what do they need? Why should they work?"

My Puritan work ethic and American sense of achievement had hit a hard cultural wall. "They don't do anything?"

Martha grinned at me. "They sit around and talk about the weather and their hunts."

"And us," said Barb. "They talk about us. We're those strange white people. They don't understand us at all."

I realized that lack of understanding was all a matter of perspective.

"We found a scorpion in our bathtub this morning," I said on our third day in Logotok. "I don't especially mind the different colored lizards running up and over the walls because I know they eat the small insects. I think I'll eventually get used to the ants and spiders, but the scorpions!"

Barb nodded. "Watch out for their stinging tails. They have one of the most painful bites there is."

"What makes the noise in the roof I hear all night?" I asked.

"Chewing?" Martha grinned. "They're totes, small, little bugs. They eat everything—mosquito nets, clothes, books, bedding. When you hear them at night, they're probably busy eating your grass roof."

"So they make the powdery dust I find everywhere in the morning." I shook my head. "If Mom could just see me now."

Another thing that took some getting used to was the nakedness of the tall, lanky Latuka men. A string of beads in the vicinity of the hips marked a well-dressed individual, though occasionally a wealthy man might actually have a piece of clothing. He might wear a pair of shorts or a T-shirt, seldom both.

"Somehow," I said, "it's not as bad as it sounds. Their blue-black skin seems a covering for them."

The married women wore animal skins from hip to hip across the back with an extra flap in front that they pushed between their legs when they sat. Until puberty girls wore nothing. Then they wore a few chains attached to a belt of cow hide slung low on their hips. During these chain years, the men and boys were not allowed to touch the girls. If they did, a costly fine of a goat or a sheep was demanded for spoiling the goods. When the girls married at about 14, they threw away the chains and wore the skins.

It seemed to me that every girl and woman over the age of four had a baby slung on her back in a sack of animal skins. The four leather strips attached to the corners of the sack were tied between the woman's breasts. It was a convenient but hot arrangement always causing the babies and women to sweat.

The little ones slept with their heads thrown back and it looked like their tiny necks would break. A hard shell made from a gourd covered the babies' heads, protecting them from the sun.

The women were beasts of burden who, in addition to the babies on their backs, always carried something on their heads, often enormous loads of grass or wood. I weighed a load of wood one day, and it weighed 80 pounds. They balanced these loads on little circlets of grass and leaves about four inches wide and an inch thick. These donuts acted as shock absorbers and allowed them to walk very gracefully and effortlessly.

Little girls began carrying small containers on their heads as soon as they could walk, gradually strengthening their neck muscles until they too were beasts of burden. The only job the young boys had was to herd the goats and cows down the mountains to pasture each day.

The men shaved their heads or cropped their hair. They pulled out all body hair including eyebrows and eyelashes. Because of this, there were terrible eye infections.

"Have you realized that there are very few Latukas with gray hair?" I asked Dallas one afternoon.

He nodded. "Short life spans."

The women also cut their hair close to their heads, but no matter how short, they always decorated their heads with brightly colored feathers, safety pins, leaves or something to make themselves more attractive. The women smoked clay pipes, using charcoal in place of tobacco. They called smoking "drinking fire."

Tribal markings scarred everyone over the age of 12. A sharp pin was used to pull up the skin into a point. Then a dirty knife or other sharp implement sliced off the skin. Manure mixed with ocher was rubbed into the wound, causing infections that in turn produced keloids or scars.

Designs were made in this manner on the face, back, chest, abdomen and upper arms. The people hardly flinched during the process, and considered them marks of great beauty. To add to their attractiveness, they also extracted the four middle bottom teeth. Both the Latuka people and their animals had their ears scalloped or notched by a rusty razor blade.

Kennie was fascinated with the spears the men and boys carried. He picked up the habit almost immediately and it was nearly impossible to keep a stick out of his hands.

On our third day, Hank Senff came to our back door.

"Winifred, this is Lodu. He's from the village and he'll help you in the house if you can take him as he is."

"As he is" meant he had never seen the inside of a white person's house, did not know what a fork or spoon was, had never seen sheets on a bed nor knew how to make one, had never washed a stitch of clothes and did not know a word of English. Worst of all, he didn't have a piece of clothing on his whole body.

The first thing I taught Lodu was how to make a bed. In sign language and by demonstration I showed him how to take the spread off the bed, fold it and then replace it. Then I let him try.

The unfamiliar task was difficult for him, but he was eager to please. He struggled for 15 minutes to get the spread off and folded and even longer to unfold it and replace it. It was weeks before he could put it on straight.

He must have thought the repetitiousness of the task foolish. He never used sheets or a spread and he slept well. We were complicating a very simple thing with our Western ways. Maybe he was right, considering the heat.

Lodu found sweeping the easiest task I asked of him. The Africans had grass brooms about 18 inches tall. Lodu swept either bent double or in a squatting position. Neither he nor the broom was as good as a carpet sweeper, but since we hadn't a carpet, they served their purpose.

If Lodu began work at 6 o'clock, he had the beds made and the floor swept by 8 o'clock. Then he would begin the laundry which he did with a washboard in half of a big metal drum. I watched him scrub away and though I'd never used a washboard either, I wondered if the task was really as hard as he made it seem. I must admit he did get the clothes clean by the simple expedient of using a whole chunk of African soap every day.

After the four hours of washing clothes came the most strenuous job of all, hanging them on the line. I taught Lodu how to hang clothes by demonstrating with a diaper.

"Shake each out," I said, shaking away. "Pull it straight." I tugged on the fabric. "Drape it on the line and put a clothespin in each corner."

Lodu used this procedure on all our clothes including our underwear. He carefully stretched the elastic as far as it would go before putting in the clothespins. The hot sun completed the deterioration of the elastic.

It was quite an experience to have the naked Lodu on the one side of the ironing board as I was on the other trying to teach him to iron. *Goya bongo* literally means "to beat the clothes." That is exactly what Lodu did as he worked with the charcoal iron. He never did learn the smooth flowing motion we associate with ironing.

After a week of "no pants," we gave Lodu a pair of shorts for which he was glad to pay the 75 cents we asked for them from his salary.

We also had Pedro to help me with the cooking. While I prepared all the food, Pedro's jobs were to keep the wood fire going and to keep things from burning. He worked in the cook house behind the main house. I had to make many trips out back to see how the meals were progressing. Pedro had a pair of tattered pants and a small pink sweater that he wore on even the hottest days.

Gerardo was our table boy, a real find who had completed second grade and knew Arabic and some English. It only took him three days to learn how to set the table, very remarkable for someone who ate with his hands.

Dallas and I listened carefully when Barb and

Martha spoke to the Latukas, but for several days we couldn't hear any distinction in words. I couldn't even hear where one word ended and another began and the tonal aspects of their speech added another mystery.

And I had thought Latin was difficult.

The Monday after we arrived, we began language study. Three of the Latukas, trained by Catholic missionaries, spoke some English and we were assigned one, Simplicio, as our teacher. Dallas was to learn Latuka so he could preach and teach while I was to learn Logotok, the local dialect and the only language the women understood.

After two weeks, we proudly said household instructions like set the table, wash the clothes or wash the dishes.

"Gerardo understood me," I said happily when the house boy went off to prepare for dinner.

"He's just being kind," Dallas said. "He knows it's time to eat."

"Well, Lodu understood this morning when I asked him to do the laundry," I said.

"When you pointed to a basketful of dirty clothes, it didn't take much imagination to get what you meant."

"Are you saying I'm not very good at Logotok?"

"About as good as I am at Latuka."

I sat in one of the two large, cushioned, Sudanese-made chairs in the living room while

Dallas sat on one of the two locally made sofa beds. In the extreme heat, we had little energy to do more. Going from cold or cool temperatures to 100 plus degrees in just the few steps it took to deplane in Juba was an unbelievable shock to all of us.

"If we could just all feel well," I said, "everything would be so much easier. There hasn't been a day since we arrived that some of us haven't been sick. Flu, fevers. I'm so worried about the kids. I can't get their fevers to go away."

"Personally, I look forward to when they sleep through the night," said Dallas. "I don't like getting up in the dark—scorpions and snakes and stuff. Even though I use the flashlight to check before I put on my shoes or step anywhere, it's hard."

"Remember how we used to just flick on a light?" I said.

We shook our heads. How far away our old life seemed. We smiled encouragingly at each other. We knew it had to get better.

First letter to my mother, January 1953:

A veteran missionary said that Sudan is the hardest field in our mission. The climate is extremely debilitating. The natives are very primitive. (They don't wear a stitch.) Transportation is most difficult and always undependable. Supplies are hard to get. Language is much more complicated than other Afri-

can languages and none of the missionaries has really learned it or written it down. We need much prayer. There has been no rain since the first of September, and the Africans cannot grow anything here but peanuts. The climate constantly drags us down.

CHAPTER 7

Sick Babies, White and Black

I learned a lot those first few weeks on the field.

I learned to boil water for 30 minutes to kill the many unseen parasites and germs after filtering it through a cloth to get out the visible dirt. We even boiled Kay's bath water.

I learned to wash, bathe and cook without a faucet, pouring water from a pitcher to a basin scores of times a day.

I learned to work a kerosene lamp and a kerosene refrigerator.

I learned to start dinner an hour earlier because the wood stove needed time to heat up and because the boys needed extra time to do their chores.

I learned a few words in Logotok and even a few in Latuka.

I learned kids' personalities alter totally in the tropics.

I learned to get over some of my fear of bugs, creeping and crawling things and chickens.

But the most important thing I learned was what it meant to have absolutely no one but the Lord to depend upon when everything seemed to be going against me.

There was the day the Reitsmas' grass-roofed house almost burned. The kids were all asleep for their afternoon naps when I looked outside. I was used to seeing the fires on the mountains at night, but this was different.

"Dallas, the fire is moving rapidly down the hill."

"Don't worry about it," he said.

"I don't think it's going to stop."

"We'll be fine."

But I wasn't sure. I dragged out a suitcase and began stuffing it with things we would need if we had to run—clothes, baby food, powdered milk. If the house did catch fire, everything would go up in a matter of minutes because of the thick dried grass roof.

Seeing my concern, Dallas walked outside to check on things, doubtless thinking he would come back and tell me I was overreacting. One look sent him shouting for Hank. They and some boys set a backfire, but even so, the advancing flames were stopped only 10 yards from the house.

"What if this had happened yesterday?" I said as we surveyed the smoldering ground. "You and Hank were both gone all day."

Dallas put his arm around me. "But it wasn't yesterday. God knew."

And then there was Kay's illness. By February 20, four weeks after we'd left New York, I was sure she had pneumonia. She wouldn't eat, drink, smile or do anything. She couldn't cry. She just mewed like a kitten, she was so blocked up. Though her temperature was only 101.6, she was a very, very sick baby and neither Martha nor I knew how to make her well.

Dear Lord, we prayed, *what should we do?*

"It's the heat here," I said. "It's too much for such a little one."

"Then we have to take her somewhere cooler," said Dallas.

Hank (Mr. "In the Congo we do it like this") suggested we go to Congo to see the excellent missionary doctor, Dr. Kleindschmidt.

"Anywhere away from this heat would be good for her," I said, "but I don't want to go as far as Congo. She needs help now."

We compromised on going to Katire Ayom where the Beattys were, only 85 miles away. They had three little children as we did, and they would know what to do. Besides, it was much cooler there. With Hank driving a half-ton pickup truck, we arrived in midafternoon to find chaos.

"We're leaving for furlough soon," Bill said, indicating the packing boxes and suitcases.

"Poor baby," said Dorothy Beatty as she looked at Kay. "I think you should take her on to Opari to see Olive Rawn. She's a great nurse, and it's only 25 miles from here."

I sagged. *Twenty-five more miles!*

"But before you go," said Dorothy, "you need something to drink." And she served us homemade root beer. We hadn't tasted anything so delicious since we'd left the States.

When we pulled into the Opari station, Olive came running. She took Kay and began penicillin treatment immediately as I hovered.

"I want you and your family to go have dinner," Olive said. "Go, Winifred. Eat and relax. And don't worry. I'll take good care of her."

"But—" I said. *How could I leave my baby?*

"Go!" Olive ordered. "You've been through a month of incredible pressure and change. I don't want you for a patient, too."

With mingled guilt and relief I left.

We had dinner that evening with Uncle John and Aunt Mabel Buyse. As the kids sat at the table, they happily exclaimed, "Oh, boy! Juice!" The water at each place was so thick with sediment that it certainly didn't resemble water.

"I'm so glad Olive can help you with Kay," said Uncle John. "And I'm so glad you arrived when you did. Olive and Betty just returned from their six-week vacation in Congo an hour before you arrived. That's why we have fresh vegetables for dinner."

"What if we had come yesterday?" I said to Dallas later. "No one would have been here."

He hugged me and said, "But we didn't. God knew."

I was learning.

The Opari station was how I pictured a mission station would look. There were three homes for the missionaries and four more for the African teachers. They taught in the school where 200 boys and a few privileged girls studied. There were three boys' dormitories, five classrooms and a dispensary. Lavender and rose bougainvillea, frangipani and beautiful red hibiscus bloomed along the paths. At the top of the hill was Olive's home, the famous "Egg," a stone building with a grass roof. It got its name from its oval shape and it was the only permanent building in our Sudan field.

The next day the Beattys drove to Opari and we had a station meeting. We, it was decided, would live at Katire Ayom in the Beattys' house while they were on furlough. We would move in about a month. Such a move meant that the Beattys would not have to pack up furniture and household items and they would know their things were safe. Plus, the Africans would know that the station was occupied. Until the move we would remain at Opari in the guest house.

I was overwhelmed at God's provision of a cooler place for us to live, and when we went to visit the Beattys to learn about their work, I knew He had given us a wonderful gift. As our kids played together, we learned that there were two native teachers and two evangelists to take care of the work. We could concentrate on language study. Someone would be brought to teach us Logotok and Latuka.

One evening I put the kids to bed and Dallas and I joined the Beattys and the visiting Reitsmas, who had returned from their medical vacation in Congo. We talked for hours. When we returned to the guest house to go to bed, I realized I'd forgotten the baby's bottle.

"I've got to go back to Beatty's for Kay's bottle," I called to Dallas. "Check on the baby, will you?"

"Where is she?" he yelled. "She's not in her bed!"

I flew back in and looked for myself at the single bed she and I had been sharing. No Kay.

"The mosquito net's pulled out!" I held it up as if Dallas hadn't already seen it. But he wasn't looking. He was reaching for Kay, asleep peacefully on the floor. As we checked our sleeping baby, it wasn't the possibility of injury from the fall that concerned us nearly as much as the dangers that lurked on the floor itself. Katire was infamous for its scorpions and any number of ants or other insects or even snakes could have bitten her. As we checked her, she wakened and smiled at us.

Oh, God! I prayed for the millionth time. *We can't be with her or the other kids all the time. Please take care of them for us! Thank You for taking care of her now.*

Life in Africa was hard on all children, but especially African children. It was not just a matter of natural enemies like scorpions, but of poor sanitation and superstition. Though they were sincerely loved, ignorance and tradition could and did harm them.

One morning Dorothy came to me.

"There's a woman in the village I'd like you to look at," she said. I nodded. I'd spent some time at the hospital at Logotok with Martha, but this would be my first trip to an African hut.

We walked about a mile on a tiny path through grass about 10 feet tall until we came to a small village. A large crowd had gathered outside one of the huts. As I walked self-consciously through the crowd, I was glad that these Acholi people, unlike our Latukas, at least wore clothes.

We bent almost double and stepped down into a dark, foul-smelling room about six feet in diameter. Cooking pots, stacks of wood, some tools and several unknowns filled the space. From pegs on the wall hung horns, axes and several spears. Stacks of drying grain lay on an overhead rack and a fire burned in a hole at the back of the hut. Huge clay pots, filled with fermenting grain, were the major source of the foul smell.

Twelve or 13 women and several men crowded the room. Most of the women were smoking their pipes and the charcoal "tobacco" gave off fumes that made my eyes water.

Squatting by the fire were two women. One of them had delivered twins nine hours earlier. The other woman, her hands dirty and bloody, faced her. Protruding from the mother's birth canal were two umbilical cords and a partially expelled placenta.

Someone talked to us and Dorothy translated:

"A boy was born first, then a girl. The placenta has come this far and no farther. Everyone's alarmed, certain that the problem was caused by evil spirits from the baby girl."

I looked at the mother squatting by the fire.

"I think her squatting position has more to do with things," I said.

We were shown the babies. I judged them to be seven or eight months gestation. The grandmother, a hard-looking, pipe-smoking woman, held the girl. The baby was gray and breathing poorly.

"She wanted to die when she was born," the grandmother said.

The boy's color was better and he seemed in fair condition. Another woman held him, trying to get him to suck from her dried-up breast.

"Lie down," I said to the patient.

Reluctantly, suspiciously she did. I palpated her uterus. It was enlarged and spongy.

As soon as I moved my hand, the woman was up again.

I took the baby girl and tried to resuscitate her.

"Please, Madame," all the women cried, "do not do anything. Let her die. She wanted to die from when she was born." And they grabbed her from me.

I sighed and turned to the patient. I gave her two doses of Ergotrate intravenously, but with no results. I felt so helpless! What could I do without instruments and cooperation?

Sadly, we left. Later we learned that the placenta was expelled after 15 hours and the mother was all right. The baby girl died and the next day the boy died also, apparently poisoned.

Letter to Grandma, March 1953:

Please, Grandma, don't worry about us. We got off to a bad start, but we are up and going again. We do not wish we were home. We are glad we are here and will be so glad when we can finally talk and really do something. I have been doing so many things here that I never did at home. By the time I come home, I'll be able to do just about anything medically. Now if I don't know how, I just act like I do and plunge ahead.

CHAPTER 8

Lifestyle Changes

Several areas of our lives had changed dramatically since we came to Africa. The most obvious was our eating habits.

For the first four or five weeks the children ate practically nothing. I don't know how they existed. Dallas and I cut down considerably too and we all lost weight. While I was glad for my loss (I was wearing a skirt I hadn't worn since our marriage), the kids didn't need to lose anything.

The heat was partly responsible for the diminished appetites; the rest was the food. Though we never went hungry, we had to learn to eat things we never would have touched back home. We ate cow's heart and sheep's lungs and other unmentionable parts of the animals. Nothing could be wasted.

We wanted to buy chickens, but no one would sell theirs. Finally we found a boy who parted with three scrawny birds. Two we kept hopefully for eggs, and the third we fattened to eat. I, who feared chickens and would never even go near a live chicken at home, walked among them, fed them and shooed them out of my way. Once when they got sick, I even gave them injections. I had the yard boy hold them and was careful never to actually touch them, but I gave them each their shots.

Fresh vegetables came in abundance whenever anyone visited Congo, but they had to be eaten quickly to beat spoilage. Any other time, canned fruits and vegetables were our only option, and they were hard to acquire and very expensive. A can that cost 10 to 25 cents in the States cost us 50 to 75 cents in Sudan. Soon every letter I wrote to Mom asked her to ship cases of canned goods and other things we couldn't readily get in Africa.

Our sleeping habits changed quite a bit too. At home we had gotten up at 7:30. In Africa we rose at 5:30 to beat the heat. Everyone but me took a siesta each afternoon, but I slept so poorly at night, I was afraid to sleep during the day lest I lie awake even longer at night. I did learn to rest during the afternoon, though, because it was the only way to survive the intense heat. The children begged to take a nap by 9 in the morning as well as taking their afternoon naps.

Our bathing habits were another thing that changed. At home Mom was always after me for using too much water. Here in Sudan the water was so limited that we all bathed in the same tubful. Before getting in, bather number four or five would often wonder, *Will I be cleaner or dirtier when I get out?* But we always bathed because of the refreshment and coolness it provided.

Washing my long, dark hair was the most difficult. The water was dirty, cloudy and extremely hard. Each hair felt as though it had been waxed when I was through washing it.

Obtaining water was always tricky. When the truck was available, a gang of school boys would ride the mile and a half to the river to haul water in quantity. When the truck wasn't available, workmen would take empty sofias, metal containers that had held four gallons of kerosene or gasoline and walk to the river. There they scooped the water, cupful by cupful, into the sofias. The men then carried the containers back on their heads. We always laughed that while we didn't have running water, we had walking water.

In dry season the small pool of water where the Africans got their water was shared with the animals that came to drink. I couldn't accept such an unsanitary situation. For us, the men dug a hole in the sand a bit farther upstream until water came seeping up through the sand.

Of all the changes that came to us in Africa, perhaps the alterations in the children delighted and concerned us most. They all tanned to a lovely shade of brown and after our original ills, looked quite healthy.

Carolyn was originally very upset over all our changes. For weeks we would just look at her and she'd start crying. Yet no matter how distressed she was, she never feared the Africans. I'd look outside and see her clasping an African child to her bosom, patting him tenderly on the head.

Kennie was stocky with a crewcut that made him look very boyish. He mimicked the Africans, loved getting dirty and was loved by everyone.

Both kids had become fussier and harder to handle. It was easy to forget that their world as they knew it had disappeared without their consent and they hadn't the adult resources to cope. It was going to take us a while to restore their equilibrium.

Kay regained all her lost weight and became her sunny self. She laughed, cooed, rolled over and loved everyone, black or white.

"It is bad, Madame," the women would tell me, "to let the baby sleep in the house. She is supposed to sleep on your back."

"She's safe," I told them. "She sleeps in a house with a door so the animals can't get in and she sleeps in a bed with a fence around it so she can't fall out. Besides Bwana is looking after her."

"Madame!" They were shocked. "Men do not know the way of feeding babies!"

Another arena in which I was aware of great

shifts was in the use of my medical training. In America a nurse was a "puppet" to do what the doctor ordered and to administer already prepared medications. In Africa a nurse diagnosed patients and prescribed medicine. She made many of the medications from scratch, including ammoniated mercury, iodoform gauze, red pepper liniment, and with a tiny scale she divided one pound packets of quinine into 10-grain piles and stuffed them into capsules. She did the lab work as well as minor—and sometimes major—surgery. She also did obstetrics.

There were many difficulties in giving medical care and aside from language, one of the biggest was my lack of familiarity with the diseases of the area. Back at Garfield Hospital, they never taught us about what I was seeing here. Even giving an IV was often difficult, done by feel because I couldn't see the veins under the dark skin and complicated by the very poor light. Further confounding things was the fact that the Africans never came to seek help until their problem was so far advanced that healing was often impossible. In the middle of March, Dallas and Uncle John went to Logotok for five days to survey and stake out the Logotok station. They were to lay out the homes, the cook houses, the church, the school and the boys' dorms. My hope was that if things were stabilized at Logotok, we would find a better balance for ourselves and the kids. Maybe we'd feel more settled and secure.

In Dallas' absence I managed the children with the help of two Acholi boys, Muganda and Aruga.

Muganda was responsible for the wash, the ironing and the bedroom jobs. He did excellent work, even ironing his own clothes with my kerosene iron. This iron was a vast improvement over the charcoal iron we'd used at Logotok, and we had fewer burn marks on our clothing.

Aruga was the "baby-boy" who helped with the children. We hadn't had a baby-boy at Logotok because I didn't feel confident enough to trust any of them with our kids. But Aruga was good, playing with Kennie and Carolyn and caring for them quite competently. The kids liked him, or rather they liked having someone to order around. Kennie liked to make Aruga carry him. The three of them did remarkably well for not knowing each other's languages.

At the end of March, Dallas left with Uncle John for Mombasa, Kenya, 1,300 miles away, to meet the boat that hauled our Carry-All and shipped goods as well as Uncle John's new truck. The five days Dallas had been away at Logotok were nothing compared to the more than three weeks he was gone this time. He and Uncle John went on faith, having no assurance that the ship actually docked on schedule and having no way of finding out.

It was just me and the three kids. What a challenge! On Sunday I took the kids to church in the mud schoolroom at Opari. At Logotok everyone met under a tree and sat on the ground. Opari seemed high civilization, having both a building and seats, forked sticks standing about a foot off the ground with two or three bamboo poles laid across them. These seats were not very comfortable for us Americans, so we brought chairs.

The service was entirely in the hands of African believers. One led the service and another preached. Church could be very boring when you don't understand a word that was said.

Still there was always something to watch. Women nursed their babies or held them out in front of them to let the little ones void on the earth floor. If a baby had diarrhea, the women called a dog lying close at hand to lick the baby's bottom. Other women sat and picked lice out of the hair of the person in front of them. Children ran in and out, jabbering to each other. Men sat and snoozed, leaning on their sticks. Chickens and dogs roamed freely.

It was not your typical United States Sunday morning church service.

Finally Dallas returned, driving our Carry-All. Since we were 70 miles from the nearest post office and more than 100 miles from the nearest store of any size, how we needed it. Finally the Green family could come and go as we pleased. Independence at last!

"The ship arrived in port the day before I got there," Dallas told us. "Talk about the Lord's wonderful timing!"

His trip to Kenya had paralleled the Mau-Mau uprisings, the most serious black/white and black/black clashes since the beginning of colonialism. Atrocities were commonplace and danger extreme. Looting and destruction of property took place everywhere, including on the mission stations. The missionaries slept with guns at their sides and ate with guns pointed at their table boys. Violence and suspicion and tragedy were everywhere.

I tried to imagine circumstances that would cause us to fear Lodu, Aruga and Muganda.

"They had to close Rift Valley Academy and evacuate the kids," Dallas said, speaking of the large school for missionary children in Kijabe, Kenya. "Uncle John and I were asked to take several kids home who lived in Congo." He shook his head. "The whole colonial system in Africa is in great danger. The nationals aren't content to be ruled anymore."

But African politics didn't interest me at the moment. Dallas was home and he had made it in time to celebrate his 30th birthday.

The day after his return we drove to Juba in our Carry-all, feeling absolutely delighted with ourselves. It only took three hours to go the 109 miles on the best road I had yet seen in Africa.

In Juba we got a hotel room, then went to the store and bought $75 worth of groceries, spending what was to us a veritable fortune. The prices of everything overwhelmed us, especially since we made the mistake of translating everything into American dollars in our minds. We bought 50 pounds of potatoes, 25 pounds of onions, 60 pounds of flour, 60 pounds of sugar and seven pounds of butter. We rejoiced over the butter, knowing that in Congo and Kenya it wasn't available. We decided against the brown sugar; it tasted like molasses.

Then we went to Sudanese customs. The Kenyans had granted entry permits for all our things, but we needed Sudanese permits also. The seven crates and barrels containing things like the children's toys, some of our clothes and some household items, were approved, though we had to pay a 20 percent duty on all new items, even things like Klim and food. The Carry-all, however, had to remain in customs until an Entry Permit was obtained.

"How long will that be?" we asked, greatly dismayed.

"Who knows?" they said.

"How about a temporary permit while we wait for the formal one?" Dallas asked.

"Not possible."

"But you can't do this to us," he said. "We need the car desperately. Besides we're United States citizens."

They shook their heads, unmoved. "No."

"But we have to get home," we said. "What should we do?"

"Who knows?" they said. What they meant was, "Who cares?"

We got a ride back to Opari with Uncle John. What a letdown after our short-lived independence euphoria.

Experiences like this brought home to us that we were the foreigners. Ours was the strange language understood only by a few. Our ways were not this culture's ways and our ways, we slowly learned, were not necessarily the right ways. Why should they listen to us, trust us, defer to us? It was very humbling and even at times humiliating.

A letter to a friend, March 1953:

Remember the time you comforted me at Vacation Bible School when Dallas left for a summer tour? He has gone again. This time it's 1,300 miles across Africa and it's three babies instead of two. He has been gone for almost three weeks and I have no way of communicating with him to know when he will return. Since our last letter to you, things have improved tremendously. We are all feeling better, so that makes the other problems of food and water seem much smaller. We rejoice in the Lord's leading and His keeping power. Truly His ways are right and even though there will be dark days ahead, God knows what He is doing, which is more than we do.

CHAPTER 9

Life at Katire

Finally, on April 13, 1953, we moved to the Beattys' house in Katire Ayom, our third home in the three months we'd been in Africa. We were very glad to be on our own in a place nicer than any so far. We had a six-room mud house with a grass roof plus use of Beattys' furniture and kerosene refrigerator. Their cook was very capable, already knowing how to make good bread. Best of all, the outdoor thermometer read a steady 90, hot but not unbearable like Logotok.

It wasn't planned for me to do medical work at Katire, but I had six patients in the first 18 hours we were there. First came a man with pneumonia, then one with a broken toe and several with malaria, pleading for *dawa* or medicine. The most challenging was a little girl who had a yellow tongue and hadn't voided for two days.

One bright, clear afternoon at the beginning of rainy season, Dallas and I took a walk while the kids napped.

"I finally feel like a missionary," I told him as we wandered to the nearest river to see if there was any water in it yet. "I finally feel we're settled enough to accomplish something."

He nodded. "Do you remember when you sang at our youth meeting about six months before we met? I said to the Lord then that if He wanted me to get married, you looked like just the kind of woman I'd like— pretty, talented and absolutely committed to God. Well, honey, God answered that wish/prayer, and I'm so glad we're in this adventure together."

Happy, having a wonderful time in spite of our tumultuous beginning, we reached the river and found a little water. About half way home, the sun disappeared and we could see the rain moving toward us as first one hill turned gray, then another. Then, whoosh! We were in it. In less than a minute we were soaked to the skin. It was wonderful.

What relief these hard, abrupt rains brought. Almost overnight, green was everywhere, so refreshing to the eyes after the dull, drab brown that had constantly surrounded us.

As the days passed, I acquired more and more patients, 18, 20, 25 a day, and I found I was learning Acholi by immersion.

"Mom," Carolyn asked me one day, "how come you have to work so hard to talk to the people? Why don't you just say it like I do?"

"I wish I could just say it like you, honey," I

said. "Unfortunately, I don't learn as quickly as you."

Eventually we invited everyone from the Opari station to come to high tea at Katire to thank them for their kindness to us. To our delight they came. I found entertaining very challenging, a matter of imagination and surmounting obstacles since there was no corner store to run to for forgotten items.

We had bought tiny hot dogs in cans, so I split them and filled them with some of my canned cheese. I made hot dog rolls from bread dough. I prepared scalloped potatoes and served peas that Dorothy Beatty had canned and left for us. I made a cake for dessert, but it flopped, so using the ice tray compartment, we made ice cream from canned milk. Since there was no kerosene refrigerator at any of the homes in Opari, the ice cream was a great treat.

Personally, it was a pleasure to serve rather than be served.

In May, after weeks alone, we suddenly had lots of company. Hank, Martha and Uncle John visited us on their way to and from various responsibilities. Fortunately Dallas was able to bag a hartebeest, so we had plenty of meat.

The big problem developed when I started to make bread. I opened a new sack of flour and found it buggy. Bags two and three were worse. The insides of the bags, which were made from a less substantial material than burlap, were covered with brown bugs and the bugs and worms were all through the flour. I was able to sift out the bugs but not the worms. I made bread anyway, but it tasted so horrible we couldn't use it.

I had to send a boy on a bicycle 25 miles to Opari for some flour, and he pedaled back the 25 miles with a large sack of flour tied to the bike. I gave him two of Kay's dresses for his daughter as a thank you.

Dallas preached his first sermon here at Katire with Musa, one of the teachers, translating for him. I sang a solo in Acholi. Then Dallas did the communion service by himself in the Acholi he had carefully memorized.

The communion wine was the real problem. We had no grape juice, only a can of pineapple juice. Then I remembered that Dorothy had left a jar of maraschino cherries. I drained off the juice, diluted it with three times the water and added some food coloring. It tasted pretty icky, but it served the purpose.

You're really a missionary, I thought, *when you compensate with whatever is at hand.*

About this time, God sent us a wonderful gift in the person of Methusala Uzele, a black missionary sent by the church in Congo to pagan Sudan. Methusala spoke eight languages, including Alure, which is similar to Acholi and fairly good English.

He helped at the infirmary by translating so I could better diagnose. He also helped in the church services, speaking, playing his trombone and interpreting for Dallas. He was really the only out-and-out African Christian we had yet met.

On May 13 we received word that our Carry-all had gotten the necessary permits to free it from customs. Hank drove Dallas to Juba to pick it up. When they arrived, they found our goods that Dallas had been unable to fit into the Carry-all on his trip to Mombasa and that he had shipped by rail and steamer. They had arrived the day prior. Again the good hand of our God was at work.

The customs official went through each item separately.

"What is a drawing board?"

"What is a T-square?"

"What is an evening gown?"

"What is a mop-head?"

Dallas tried to explain each, a difficult task, especially the last to a people whose floors were dirt.

On another trip to Juba Dallas collected our tool chest and typewriter and a wonderful gift, a hand-operated sewing machine. I found sewing with my right hand constantly on the wheel and only my left hand to control the fabric a bit of a challenge, but how it speeded up things! I made a net for Kay's crib in only a few hours and later I made nets for Carolyn and Kennie's beds.

I needed the machine to replenish or repair our clothes. They were disintegrating rapidly from being washed with bar soap on a wash board. There were also Lodu's burn marks and the evidences of the insects' appetites pocking the fabric. Also, especially when we were still in Logotok, our clothes disappeared from the clothesline.

It was amazing how a person wearing no clothes and carrying no bag could make off with something. He would discreetly remove the item from the line, roll it up and put it under his armpit, walking away with no one noticing a thing.

This lack of a sense of ownership among the pagan people was trying. Stealing something was perfectly acceptable unless you got caught. Things that were locked up were available by the simple expedient of knocking off the padlock.

But fun things happened, too. One time when Dallas was away on a short safari, we heard a truck. Three men from the Sudan Public Relations Department got out and set up movie equipment from the Cinema Department. Using a generator on the truck they showed movies to the people that night.

What a scream! Everyone laughed and laughed as they watched a movie about a London aerodrome, another on the care of teeth, another about a trip on the Nile and a fourth about fishing on the Nile.

What, I wondered, did these people who had never left their village think about a river the size of the Nile or a place like a London airport? They did brush their teeth using a stick that was chewed until the end was frayed and soft. However, what did they think about a toothbrush and paste?

While we lived at Katire we attempted to learn Latuka for the time we would return to Logotok. What a strange sounding language it was! I got so I could read and understand some of it, but I certainly couldn't speak it. The words still seemed to run into each other, and everything sounded like a version of *is* or *ess* or *te*.

Trying to find appropriate words for translating Scripture and biblical concepts was a constant struggle. Martha and Dallas dug and dug into the vocabularies of dozens of boys, trying to find a word that could translate *Holy Spirit*. The closest they came was *clean shadow*, which was far from the mark. In Acholi, the word for *God* was *chief*, and in Latuka it was *creator*, but they used the same word for *evil spirits*.

Martha, the linguist among us, translated first the Gospel of Mark, then the Gospel of John, always working to improve their clarity. Our Bible teaching was limited to these two books. In some ways, it didn't really matter because we gave the same message over and over each day at the dispensary. *God loves you, but you are a sinner separated from God by your sin. He sent Jesus to be the sacrifice for your sin. Believe in Jesus and be saved.* Even so, I'm sure the majority of the patients couldn't understand our poor language delivery.

I started a school for the women at Katire, and usually eight came. Though class started at three, they arrived anywhere within an hour of that stated time. They kept time by the sun, and they weren't as punctual as we missionaries with our watches.

To interest the women in the class, I taught them to make skirts. I used the muslin my mother wrapped around all our packages from home. Class went well for the short time until the rains began. Then everyone took off to work in their gardens and my school died.

One Sunday we drove 15 miles and Dallas preached to 70 people. The gospel had never been preached in that village before. What a thrill to be the first to tell them of God's Son. We had the service in the open courtyard. People wandered around, talking, dancing, smoking. It was not very pious.

But we were doing "real" missionary work.

From a letter to my Grandpa, the civil engineer, Spring, 1953:

Grandpa, you would really get a bang out of these roads. They have what are called "Irish bridges" at the rivers. They are cement or broken rock paths following the contours of the riverbeds. The water goes over instead of under the bridge when it rains. This way the bridges don't need supports. When it does rain, the rivers swell and we sit for hours or overnight until the water goes down. There are Irish bridges even on good roads. On the Logotok road we wish there were Irish bridges because we have to make our own road after each rain.

CHAPTER 10

Move In and Out of Logotok

All of our children had had health problems ever since we arrived in Africa, but Kay had become our greatest concern. She turned eight months old on June 21, but she was only the size of a five-month-old, 15 pounds. She did pull herself up in her playpen and had begun to stand alone. Still she hadn't gained weight for three months, and she vomited constantly.

What do we do? we prayed.

"What do we do?" we asked our colleagues.

"Go see Dr. Becker in the Belgian Congo," they said.

On Thursday, July 2, we left for Rethy, Congo, 380 miles away, to visit the doctor. We drove south into Uganda, then west to Congo. In Sudan and Uganda, people had British vehicles and drove on the left side of the road. When we entered Congo, we immediately noticed all the

American Chevrolets, Mercurys and Buicks and we had to switch to the right side of the road. The roads were wonderful.

What a revelation the trip was! It was my first time to see Africa beyond our section of Equatoria Province. The farther we got from Sudan, the more we saw "normal" (as in Western) life—cottages, flowers, palm and banana trees, electricity and glass windows. At the mission station at Aru, Congo, we saw a brick church with a platform and a pulpit, a good-sized hospital and schools for both boys and girls.

When we arrived at Rethy, we found fresh vegetables: beautiful lettuce and cauliflower, peas, beets, carrots, cabbage and even sugar cane. And flowers! We saw dahlia beds a block long, and large plots of roses and carnations bloomed everywhere.

It was so cold in Rethy that we slept under blankets and kept a fire in the fireplace of the mission guest home all day. It was lovely. And there was fresh beef and pork to eat every night as we ate with different missionaries.

We remained in Rethy for five days waiting for Dr. Becker. He made a circuit each month of the various mission stations, operating and seeing the most difficult cases. When he saw Kay, he said he wanted to see her longer than just in passing. Would we please go on to Oicha, his home base?

So we drove 245 more miles through fields of

pineapples, groves of lemon, tangerine and banana trees and forests of mahogany. I hadn't seen things this lovely since I'd arrived in Africa.

At Oicha we lived in a four-room, brick guest house with mahogany doors and furniture. It was lovely as was Dr. Becker's house.

"Dallas, it's all so wonderful! The surroundings, the house, the food, the ministry here. I can't believe it."

"It is a contrast to Sudan," he said in understatement. "We've got to keep reminding ourselves that all we see is the result of 30 years of hard work."

"So Sudan can be like this in 30 years?"

Dallas hesitated. "Different culture. Different climate. Different people."

"But the same God," I said.

"The same God," he agreed. "We'll leave the 'success' of the Sudan work to Him and enjoy the luxuries of the Congo while we can."

Dr. Becker had the largest leper camp in the world, over 3,000 inhabitants. He had thousands of other ill people coming to the dispensary every day, and he had trained more than 35 Africans to do the work. They saw and diagnosed most of the patients and helped in surgery. Specially trained African evangelists presented the gospel to all the out-patients and visited each hospital patient to talk about salvation.

"We need something like this in Sudan," I

said as I stared at the hospital in awe.

"If we can ever master the language," Dallas said, his pastor's heart taken with the national evangelists. "But what a goal to have!"

Dr. Becker put Kay on a new formula, a new medication and a new feeding schedule. We had to awaken her at night to feed her. Soon she began gaining weight, though she still regurgitated some. We stayed at Oicha for two weeks, the first vacation we had had since our marriage. The cooler weather and the good food helped not only the children but Dallas and me. We drove back to Sudan much refreshed and ready to move back to Logotok.

On September 5 we moved into two rooms of the new storehouse. The two rooms in which the five of us lived were 12 by 13 feet and 12 by 6 feet. Our house was still not completed, mainly because Dallas was needed on site to keep the work going.

Everything we owned, transported from Katire in six trips, was stored in the four unfinished rooms of the storehouse. Its walls were of handmade, burned bricks with a coat of mud smeared over them inside. A second layer of sand and ashes was smoothed over the mud, making it look like block plaster.

I had hoped for ceilings in our home and I got my wish, making ours the only missionary house in south Sudan with ceilings. The ceilings were made by attaching strips of bamboo to the top of the walls and crisscrossing them over each other. Mud was then pushed through from above and another layer was pushed through from below. The window frames, built by Dallas at Katire and transported to Logotok for installation, were full size with screens, not glass. Mud filled the cracks between the walls and the windows.

The house was tiny, but I felt it was the nicest house in our Sudan field.

We also built a "little house" or outhouse. Like all other buildings, it had a grass roof and mud walls. The men dug a hole 23 feet deep. So we could use this most necessary facility while the work was in progress, three logs were balanced across the great hole and a box with a hole in the middle was placed on the logs. I used it with great caution and trepidation until they put in the log floor covered with mud. I went out just after they finished work on the floor and sank to my ankles in the fresh mud.

Carolyn turned four on September 29 and we had a party for her. It was the first day since our move to Logotok that my stove was usable and the first day for Georgio, my new cook. When he first applied for the job, I was taken by his smile and told him he could have the job if he got some pants.

His first responsibility was Carolyn's birthday cake. I used a white and a chocolate mix and made marble cake. Georgio and I wore ourselves out beating the mixes by hand the required number of times, and he enthusiastically heated the oven to 400 degrees. The cake was light as a feather and disintegrated at our touch. I stuck it together with straws made from bamboo strips and cemented it with icing, but it was a mess and tasted like cardboard.

Carolyn was delighted, though; and enjoyed her party. For weeks she had been asking, "Is it my birthday yet?" When the great occasion finally arrived, she reveled in the special attention. Martha, Barb, Hank and the Reitsmas—Kim, Doug and Susie—came to celebrate with us. Carolyn got a dress, some small gifts and a doll whose eyes wouldn't open. They probably got stuck while in storage in one of our barrels. Several weeks later I happened to hit the doll just right and the eyes popped open, much to Carolyn's delight.

We had barely begun to settle in at Logotok when the most surprising thing happened. We were asked to move again, this time to Opari.

"This will make five moves in nine months," I said to Dallas, "if you don't count the trip to Congo, which I guess you don't because it was really vacation."

He looked at me cautiously. "How upset are you?"

I shook my head. "I'm not upset. I just want to get somewhere and stay there!"

"We'll be there for a year," Dallas said. "Doug asked if you'd take Olive's place at the Opari dispensary while she's on furlough."

"We were supposed to be at Beattys' during their furlough, but we only stayed a couple of months."

"This is different," Dallas assured me. "It's a matter of real need."

"Oh, I understand the reason for the move. Here in Logotok we have three nurses and a doctor. At Opari they only have Olive and she's about to leave." I took a deep breath and voiced my greatest concern about the new plan. "What about the kids? I can't do the dispensary and care for them as I should."

"I'll watch the kids until we can make other arrangements," Dallas said.

"You? But what about your work? What about your preaching and language study?"

"I can still study Latuka and Acholi. Right now the nursing is more important than the preaching, especially considering my language expertise."

"Are you sure you don't mind staying home while I'm working?"

"I honestly don't. I'm glad you have the skills to be so useful. And it won't be for too long."

I stared at Dallas. It was one thing to be verbally supportive of your wife, her work and her ministry, and quite another to stay home with three little kids while she went off each day.

"Honey," Dallas said, "I'm willing to do what's best for the work of the Lord in Sudan. I'll get plenty of chances to preach before we're done here."

"OK," I said. "If that's how you really feel, we'll do it."

By late October we were at Opari where we celebrated Kay's first birthday with a party that included a cake that turned out beautifully and limeade made from real limes grown on our own trees.

Kay was finally growing and had taken to pushing her bottle through the slats of her crib onto the cement floor. The day she broke her last bottle, I held my breath. She refused to drink from a cup for six hours, became desperate, tried the cup and never looked back. She was walking all over the house and was trying to talk. We delighted in her health and spirits.

The night before my first day at the dispensary, I sat in the living room in a mild panic. "I feel as dumb as I did my first day as a student nurse," I said. "There's so much I don't know! And so much responsibility! Back at Garfield Hospital they never let us do stuff like I'm going to have to do. And what do I really know about tropical diseases?"

"You'll be fine, honey," Dallas assured me. "No matter how little you know, you know more than they do."

I thought back to Logotok when I had been sent for in the night to see a sick man. I had walked the dark trail alone, afraid but determined, the myriad stars suspended in the black sky lighting my way. I'd never really seen stars until I'd come to Africa, but here millions flashed every night. The Southern Cross hung outside our front door and the North Star outside the back. When there was no moon, the night was black as pitch. When there was a full moon, you could read by it.

That night by starlight I'd found a man who looked sick but acted very strangely.

He's not really ill, I thought skeptically. *It's something else.* I treated him quickly and went home.

I found out the next day I was right. While he had a touch of malaria, he was suffering mostly from drunkenness and too much sun. He was well enough to beat his wife that very night.

Well, Lord. You got me through that situation and many others. You can get me through tomorrow.

I had 117 patients my first day running the dispensary and the numbers escalated. In October, Olive and I together had 2,571 patients and in November I saw 2,340 by myself. I kept reading the medical books, praying like crazy, doing my best.

I found myself treating threatened miscarriages, amoebic dysentery, leopard bites, malaria, starving babies and pneumonia. I did no bedside nursing like bed baths or back rubs or changing beds. No time, no beds.

"Dallas, I'm so unprepared," I said over and over. "I don't know tropical medicine. I don't know what I'm doing."

"Next time we have vacation, we'll go to Congo again," he said. "There you can observe in some of the hospitals and learn."

"Can we really do that?" *What a wonderful thing to look forward to. What a wonderful husband.*

At the beginning of November, Dallas was appointed station superintendent. Because we had found a girl to watch the children and because I now had a set schedule at the dispensary, Dallas was free to pursue his various responsibilities, which he did with great enthusiasm.

At the dispensary I got a lot of burn cases. To stay warm the people kept fires burning in their huts all night. The mothers slept on the floor with the babies snuggled against them. Often the babies rolled into the fire in their sleep. Two babies had severe head burns, their whole heads a mass of red flesh. For other burned babies I had to amputate toes and fingers because they were so badly injured.

I gave all the babies I treated liquid medicine, but getting them to swallow it was quite a chore. Since all my patients sat under a big tree while they waited for treatment, they helped one another. A mother would hold her baby in her arms and two others would hold his hands and feet. Then I, a white woman with long dark hair, wearing a white uniform, would lean over the screaming child and put strange tasting *dawa* in his mouth.

Everything about me was so different from their naked black mothers.

Invariably the terrified baby spat the stuff out, often in my face. The mother would then take her filthy, dirty finger and scrape as much of the medicine as she could off the baby and push it back in his mouth. Eventually the baby got to know me well enough not to struggle and he would accept the medicine I offered. Miraculously most of the children became well.

I often equated that experience to God and me. He wants to teach me something and I struggle and complain until He has to hold me down and pour the medicine down my throat. I become frightened because His ways are so different from mine. I rebel and tell God that He doesn't know what He's doing. Then, as I get to know Him better, it's easier to accept the hard things in my life. I learn I can trust Him through the hardship and pain, the changed plans. I accept that "God's ways are not my ways" and that "all things work together for good" for me as His child. Such personal lessons were a large part of our African experience.

In the middle of this caring for other people's children, our own once again concerned us greatly.

One night Kennie spiked a fever of 103 and went into convulsions that lasted 20 minutes. Then he was unconscious for three hours. We worked over him, gave him warm baths and covered him with blankets. We felt so alone and so vulnerable.

He was not himself for a long time after that seizure.

At the same time, Carolyn came down with malaria. Both she and Kennie had constant diarrhea. While we rejoiced that Kay was finally growing, we worried over the other two.

Then at Thanksgiving I became ill. We were to entertain all the Opari missionaries for the holiday now that we were settled into Olive's comfortable, ceiling-less house, the famous Egg. I had planned everything so carefully. However, I did little of the cooking. Betty Wilson cooked two of our chickens and Aunt Mabel made the dressing. We were to have mashed potatoes, a precious can of tomatoes and even more precious cans of corn and lima beans. I baked pies earlier. As it turned out, everyone had a wonderful dinner but the hostess. I was flat on my back with a sudden attack of malaria.

I couldn't decide which was worse, the pills to treat the disease or the malaria itself. At least I had finally found something to make me vomit. I had been nauseous for the entire nine months of each pregnancy, but it took malaria to make me actually throw up. And that was only part of the misery. There were also fever, chills, sweats, shaking, cramps, diarrhea and generalized aches.

Oh, Lord, I thought, *how come we're always*

getting sick like this? We take the preventive medication just as we're supposed to. And the kids, Lord! Do they have to be so ill? Were we wrong to bring them here?

But I saw a clear picture of the situation. It was our health and comfort versus the eternal destiny of the people of south Sudan. How could we choose to do other than stay and trust ourselves and our kids to God's care?

Letter to Mom, November 1953:

Here is one for your dinner table talk. Several times lizards 13 to 15 inches long have fallen from the grass roof above us and landed near us. One night, sitting in our front room, one fell right in front of me and missed me by an inch. Tonight at dinner, one landed ker-plunk right beside Dallas' plate. They fall 15 feet, so make quite a thud or splash. It's not that they are an oddity because we see them crawling up the walls and around the floor, but we do not relish lizard soup.

By the way, when you send fabric, don't send anything with a white background. The water is so muddy and dirty that things become discolored their first washing.

CHAPTER 11

At Home Where the Buffalo Roam

Our first Christmas in Africa was fast approaching, and I rejoiced at the arrival of Mom's boxes of gifts. Her Sunday school class had had a Christmas party in August and all the women had brought a gift for each of our children. They had wrapped and packed them that very night.

No one wrapped things like Mom. She chose strong cardboard boxes, wrapped the box in paper, then sewed it in unbleached muslin. Then she added another layer of sturdy brown paper.

I decided to look through the boxes to decide which toys to give the kids and which ones to save for later occasions. I was struck with how soft every item within the boxes was to the touch, even what appeared to be toy cars and trucks.

Then I remembered a line in one of Mom's

letters: "I packed everything in Kotex."

Am I glad I remembered! I opened all the packages and ended up with quite a supply of Kotex for which I was thankful. Then I re-wrapped the gifts the kids would receive, so grateful for escaping the potential embarrassment to all the guests, especially the men, we were to have Christmas morning.

We started our Christmas celebration two days before Christmas when the five of us toured our yard looking for a tree. The fires had burned most of the trees, but we found a fine, eight-foot tree with wide, flat leaves about nine inches long. We checked with Uncle John, and he said it was teakwood and we could cut it down.

Later that day Betty came to the door and called, "Hodi!"

"Come see our Christmas tree," I said. "Dallas and the kids are setting it up in the living room."

"Great! But first, what happened to *my* tree?" she asked, pointing to the stump at the far edge of the compound yard. "Did you see who chopped it down? And I ask you—why couldn't they take the brush and trees on the mountain if they needed firewood? Why my tree?"

"Your tree?" I said weakly.

She nodded. "It's a cashew. I planted it a few years ago. I've been babying it along."

"Uncle John said it was teakwood."

"Teakwood?" She shook her head in disbelief. "He should know better. It just isn't bearing fruit right now." She stopped abruptly, looked at my guilty face, and sighed. "Your Christmas tree is my cashew?"

We decorated it anyway.

"Might as well," Dallas said. "We certainly can't replant it."

We used paper decorations I had made before Dallas and I were married. Everyone said it was the best tree in the history of the Sudan field.

It was important for me to make Christmas as much like home as I could. I wanted our kids to have a feel for what happened in America, and the only way that would happen was if we created islands of home here at Opari.

Kennie and Kay were too young to have many memories of home, and those Carolyn had were fast fading.

Someone had sent me a subscription to *Good Housekeeping*, and Carolyn loved to leaf through, studying the pictures.

"Is this lipstick the ladies are wearing?" she asked timidly, remembering from home. "Why do they wear it?"

"To make their lips redder," I said, thinking of my unrouged lips. No self-respecting missionary would wear lipstick, but it still seemed so American. And my kids were losing the sense of American.

So I planned Christmas carefully. For dinner

Christmas Eve we had Uncle John and Aunt Mabel, Betty Wilson and Jean and Dan Olsen, new missionaries at Opari. We had a small canned ham that had come in the boxes from home and a small dik-dik that Dallas had hit with the car. I served mashed potatoes, candied native potatoes, canned corn and lima beans and that most American dish, cranberry sauce, also sent from home. The rolls I made with the last of my American flour tasted especially good. For dessert we had butterscotch pie, tropical pie and a fruit cake, also from home.

After dinner we butchered two cows for the Africans' feast the next day. Then the girls from Betty's school came and caroled for us. They only knew two carols, but they sang them well. The boys beat the drums all night in honor of the celebration and we didn't get much sleep. Still at 6:30 Christmas morning when our guests returned, we enjoyed watching the kids open their presents.

They opened their slippers first and were so happy with them. They went wild over their toys and clothes, especially the wading pool someone in Mom's class had sent. I wasn't sure that the water shortage would allow us to use it, but if we could manage, it would be far better than the little metal tub I sometimes used.

At 9, we went to church and celebrated the Lord's Table. When that was over, we went outside and held a service for the Africans. Dallas planned and led it. Jean Olsen and I sang

"Joy to the World" in Acholi. We had about 500 in attendance, a super crowd.

Next we invited our houseboys—who all had the day off—to come to our home with their wives and children. We gave them all a little cloth sack for their Acholi New Testaments. In the sack we put an orange, a piece of candy, a stick of chewing gum, a balloon, a picture, a card with two safety pins, two needles and five straight pins and the equivalent of 30 cents. We gave each of the children a toy from our kids' supply. They were all very well pleased.

Later there was an afternoon of games for the Africans including all kinds of races, tug-of-war, high jump, tire rolling contests and football. Dallas had planned that, too, and everyone had a fine time.

The new year came and my medical work continued. One day a man gored by a buffalo was brought in. The animal's horn had caught him in the chest and twirled him around before dropping him on the ground. The man's rib cage was torn open and I could see his lungs and heart pulsating underneath. Taking a deep breath, I sewed him up as best I could. He bled a little, but seemed to recover well.

Another buffalo story didn't have the same happy ending.

"Madame, Bwana," the Africans called as they ran to our house one afternoon. "There's a buffalo just over the hill behind your house. Come and kill it with your gun."

"Not now," Dallas said.

Soon there were 50 people outside, all wanting the buffalo killed for the meat.

Suddenly someone said, "Lakana has been gored by the buffalo."

Lakana was our garden boy and an outstanding Christian. The crowd as a whole wasn't too concerned about Lakana or his health; they just wanted the meat. To us, however, Lakana was very important. Dallas got him in the truck and met me at the dispensary.

What a sight! On Lakana's right thigh was a huge mass of muscle as large as my two fists, bulging outside the skin. His leg was broken mid-thigh and at the knee. He had cuts and bruises all over from the buffalo trampling him. To complicate things, Lakana was on daily medication for epilepsy.

I injected novocaine around the wound, put on my gloves and started. It took every bit of strength to push the muscle back in and close the wound around it. I also feared he would have a convulsion any minute. I gave him penicillin, sulfa, aspirin and phenobarbital. I straightened his leg and splinted it with two of Dallas's precious two-by-fours he planned to use for building.

Then Dallas took him to the doctor's in Torit 60 miles away. Poor Lakana died about halfway there but Dallas took him on anyway. The doctor said he died of internal bleeding from the trampling.

Dallas then drove Lakana 50 miles farther to his village. There he led the first Christian funeral in the history of our Sudan field. It made a great impression on the people in spite of their wailing and other heathen practices.

Dallas knew the language much better now and he preached whenever he could. He held a series of evangelistic meetings in one of the villages. The first night only 46 came. The second night about 200 attended and the third night over 600 heard the gospel. Though the attendance was good, there was little response, not an unusual occurrence.

We were never certain how much the people understood when we preached. Between the language problems and the complexity of the ideas involved, preaching wasn't as easy as it sounded and explaining biblical truths with clarity was difficult. Of the 46 we had baptized at Christmas, all but two appeared to have abandoned their faith, if faith they had, running off to the beer-dances and other activities inconsistent with living a Christian life. We were heartbroken.

"Did they ever actually trust the Lord?" I asked. "Did they understand what they heard you say?"

Dallas shook his head. "I don't know. I just don't know."

"I was so naive," I said. "I expected that everyone in Africa was just waiting to hear about Christ and that they would flock to Him."

We looked across the brutal African land-scape.

"People didn't accept what Paul preached," Dallas said, squinting against the sun. "They didn't even believe Jesus Himself. We shouldn't be surprised when they don't rush to commit to the Lord when I preach."

I nodded. I knew that. But some days when I thought of all we had given up, I wished for a bit more appreciation from the people we had given it up for. Instead, they saw us as the "half-baked ones" with our white skin and strange habits and seeming wealth. They kindly offered a passive acceptance to us and an indifference to the Lord.

Even when they came to us for medicine, it was usually after trying their witch doctor first. When there was no help there, then they would come to *Akim*, the white doctor or nurse.

But we knew we were in Satan's domain, and every so often we were forcefully re-minded of that fact.

Dallas was preaching in an outlying village when about 100 warriors incited the people against him.

"Out!" they screamed. "Get out! Leave us!"

The crowd surged forward, forcing Dallas and his interpreter to flee before their anger.

"We don't want you here! Get out!"

As Dallas drove away, his interpreter got on the roof of the van and yelled, "We are going, but you will hear one thing before we go."

Whether the people could hear him over the chaos didn't concern the man. He had something to say and he would say it.

"We did not come to take water and food or to take houses and lands. But we came to tell you of Jesus, the Son of God, who died and rose again for you. And we will be back."

Prayer letter, January 26, 1954:

"A home where the buffalo roam" can be yours if you wish to venture out to our south Sudan field.

A whole year has passed since we left the States. A hard year? Yes! Extremely so, with sickness and acclimatizing, moving about from station to station, learning so many different things. In spite of all these things, how wonderfully the Lord has provided, supplied and cared for us. We count on your continued prayer support.

CHAPTR 12

Water and Crime at Opari

The most wonderful thing occurred on our south Sudan stations in early 1954. We finally had wells and the clear, clean water they produced.

Earl Dix, a missionary in neighboring Congo, came to south Sudan with well-drilling equipment purchased by a Christian man in New York. The express purpose of the drilling was to obtain the enduring water resources the government required to grant us permanent mission sites.

Mr. Dix had never drilled a well before and the project was a work of God in the fullest sense. Wisdom to use the sophisticated equipment, safety for all the novice workers and the selection of the actual well sites were matters of great amounts of prayer. And God answered.

At Opari, Mr. Dix and his team dug a bore hole six inches in diameter down over 100 feet through granite before they reached water. The granite was so hard they had to stop every few feet to sharpen the bits by heating them and then beating them with a sledge hammer to restore the cutting edge.

Even after our centrally located well was drilled, getting water was hard work because of the long, heavy pump handle. The water boys struggled with its weight. After they pumped a sofia full, they carried it to the house and stored the water in 55 gallon drums. Clear as the water was, we continued to boil any used for drinking and cooking rather than take chances with the invisible bugs that swam hungrily in it.

During well drilling time, we had many extra people for meals. It was hard on our sparse supply of food and on our houseboys.

People were always writing to ask about our "servants." We had 13 boys on our payroll: one cook, one table boy, one bedroom boy, two who helped at the dispensary, two wood boys, and six water boys. I imagine people thought I did nothing all day since I had all this help. Right.

Moi, my cook, had five years experience cooking for various missionaries and did very well. Each morning when I left for the dispensary, I would tell him what to cook.

One day during the well drilling, I said, "Make the bread of the pie (that's the crust) and black milk pudding (that's chocolate pudding). Cut up

116

a few bananas and put them on top of the bread of the pie. Pour the black milk pudding over them."

Moi produced a wonderful looking dessert. I cut and served it with pride.

"This looks delicious," said my guests as they eagerly took large pieces. "We haven't had anything like this for so long!"

Then they took a bite. We found out quickly that the big lumps in the bottom of the pie were not bananas but uncooked bacon.

"Moi, what happened?" I asked.

What happened was my pronunciation. *Banana* and *bacon* sound exactly the same except for the fact that one goes up tonally at the end and the other goes down. I had said the right word the wrong way.

It's hard to scrape chocolate pudding off soft bacon hunks.

Another evening the pie crust was quite crunchy.

"Coconut, Winifred?" one of the guests asked. "What a nice idea."

Unfortunately it wasn't coconut. It was bugs and worms that had sifted through with the flour. Just a little extra protein for my visitors.

The next day I gave Moi a cake mix to make. He mixed it like always, put it in the oven and went home. So much for that cake. The following night, again with guests and workers at our table, Moi put part of the dinner on the stove and walked off, never to return again.

Ah, the joys of having "servants."

Another time we had 16 of the girls from Betty's school, who walked 16 miles, come to work for us while she was on vacation. They quickly found they weren't happy with the demands of our busy household. Caring for Betty, a single individual who excused their failures graciously, was very different from two busy adults and three noisy, active children.

Betty's girls wanted to do every job together, whether it was wash clothes or dishes, make beds or set the table. What a commotion. And how slowly everything got done.

We also had some unusually demanding and heavy work to be done at that time as we were moving into Betty's larger house and we painted it before our move. On moving day the girls carried all our belongings on their heads in a long and noisy procession down the hill.

Then, too, there was the matter of the girls and school. They had come to Opari to attend the boys' school. We were to pay their fees in exchange for their work for us. At Betty's school, if the girls hadn't finished their housework in time for class, Betty would adjust her schedule for them. When they attended the boys' school, they had to be prompt for classes. They had difficulty adjusting to this inflexible schedule.

One evening after they had worked for us for just a few days, they took out our bath water, together as always. A half hour later I called them for prayers. Nobody responded. When we checked, we found their dorm empty. They had decided they didn't like the pressures, jumped a passing cotton truck, and gone home without a word to us.

"We failed Betty." I felt terribly guilty.

Dallas shrugged. "Maybe it was our fault. Then again maybe it was the girls' fault."

"It was us," I said. "I know it. We failed."

"Honey, don't be so hard on yourself. It's OK"

But I felt guilty for a long time.

As we prepared to move into yet another new-to-us house, I decided that the fresh native whitewash applied to the mud walls both inside and out wasn't enough.

"We'll paint the walls for more color," I said, and I ordered enough powdered green paint from Sears to cover eight walls.

When it came, we mixed it in large tubs of water according to the directions. It was a warm, wonderful green and I was excited. The next instructions were: "Remove all dirt from the walls." Obviously the paint wasn't developed with mud houses in mind.

Dallas began to paint and the mud walls greedily sucked up the moisture. Instead of eight walls of color we got three. But what a beautiful improvement they were to our house!

I tried another experiment in an attempt for more color. I added a bottle of blue ink, some laundry bluing and a bottle of blue food coloring to the whitewash itself. We were so happy as we put the glorious blue wash on the wall. How American it looked!

Imagine our surprise the next morning when we found our blue walls had become merely a whiter white overnight. I think I shouldn't have added the laundry bluing.

I decided to become content with the white-washed walls and I added color in brightly patterned drapes and pictures from magazines.

Shortly after the well drilling, our move and the girls' disappearance, we spent a week on the road, visiting mission stations in Uganda and Congo. The sophistication of the work and the beauty of the stations were overwhelming. We went to Rethy, Congo, and I studied tropical medicine under Dr. Barnett for a few days.

I also canned fresh pork and vegetables to take back to Opari. We gathered seeds, bulbs and a pair of rabbits to take home too. Unfortunately, nothing grew, including the rabbits.

Our kids were growing and they copied the Africans more and more. One day I came upon Carolyn on her hands and knees, doll tied on her back, bending over the grinding stone. With great pushes and pulls she crushed some real grain she had found. She was making flour and catching it in a little gourd cup, just like the Africans.

Kay, kneeling at a nearby stone, was trying to do the same thing but she wasn't strong enough to crush the grain. Kennie was between them, winnowing the grain and pouring little handfuls of good kernels on the girls' grinding stones.

As I continued to watch, the kids took two sticks and pulled live coals from the cook stove. They carried them outside and built a fire on which they cooked their flour and water.

Oh, Lord, I prayed then as I did so often, *thank You for the great joy they give us. Please keep them safe and well!*

About this time a man came to the dispensary with his right thigh ballooned out to twice its normal size.

"Someone put poison on my stool," Ocher told me.

Whatever had happened, it was one of those times I acutely felt my lack of training and wished fervently for a doctor.

First, I cut up some rubber gloves and made drains that I inserted at various places in the thigh. Then I worked every day trying to clean the huge wound, at times removing repulsive, squirming maggots with the gangrenous tissue.

Eventually I had to remove all the skin and most of the muscle from hip to knee. I performed this surgery under a tree while Ocher's wife shooed flies with a bundle of leaves.

After a month, the leg was ready for plastic surgery.

"What do I do now?" I said. "I can't do the type of surgery Ocher needs now."

"Good news," Dallas said. "I just heard there's a surgeon on temporary duty at the government hospital 60 miles away. We can take him there."

Delighted as I was that Ocher was to get the help he needed, we were more delighted that he had trusted Christ as his Savior. Daily for all those weeks, he had listened to the gospel presentation and believed.

"I was dead," Ocher told me, "but now I am alive in Jesus."

Interestingly, *Ocher* means resurrection.

One day a man came in from the bush.

"I have seen an antelope," he said, clearly wanting Dallas to go shoot it.

Meat was always an interesting problem in south Sudan, a matter of feast or famine. Every two or three months when we did have meat, we ate it three times a day because we could store or can very little of it.

Dallas went out to look for the antelope and after a short search shot two water bucks about the shape and size of a donkey. We stored as much of the meat as we could in the small freezer compartment of our kerosene refrigerator. We divided the rest between the boys' school and our house boys. Everyone was delighted because the meat was quite good.

The next week on the way back from Torit, Dallas shot a hartebeest weighing about 300 pounds. Such plenty was overwhelming and you'd think that after all this time I would have gotten hardened to the sight of wild meat in the rough.

"You see and do bloody things at the hospital all the time, honey," Dallas always teased me. "What's there to get upset about in a leg of meat, even if the muscles are still twitching?"

"Take my word for it," I said. "There's a difference."

Still, necessity forced me to become an amateur butcher. Where at home we'd bought liver by the quarter pound, here I got the whole thing. At home filet mignon went for an enormous price per pound; here it was the only tender part of the animal and we used it for steaks and roasts. Everything else was ground in a small, hand-operated meat grinder, a very lengthy process because the tendons of the wild meat were so tough that the grinder couldn't chew them. We had to take it apart every few minutes and clean it.

It was late spring 1954 that we made two special purchases. First, we bought a pair of elephant feet, approximately 22 inches wide and a foot high, each with a piece of polished wood across the top. They were designed to be used as stools.

"Now that's Africa," Dallas said to the British officer from whom we bought them. The officer was selling most of his belongings, preparing to leave Sudan in the summer when the government passed into national hands.

A few weeks after we bought the elephant feet, we saw a cloud of dust on the road, and soon the officer was standing at our door.

"My wife has written me from England," he said. "The one thing she has told me to be sure to bring home with me is the elephant feet."

"Well," said Dallas, thinking quickly, "I'll sell you one and keep one."

"Done!" said the officer.

Our other purchase was a piano. The British District Commissioner told Dallas about one available in Katire Gilo, 100 miles northeast. When we finally managed to make the trip to get it, we were so surprised to find such a beautiful spot in Sudan. Located in a forest up in the mountains, Katire Gilo was surrounded by mahogany, olive and teakwood trees and an abundance of flowers. The altitude was 6,300 feet and the climate wonderfully cool.

The piano was a spinet owned by a British government official about to go on furlough. We packed the piano carefully with burlap bags and quilts and drove 10 miles an hour over the deplorable roads where the mountain descended 3,500 feet in 15 miles.

The piano survived the trip very well and the next day the owner visited to tune it for me. He left the homemade tuning device for me after teaching me how to use it.

We paid $290.00 for the piano. Our understanding was that when the man and his family returned from furlough in a year, they would purchase it back for the same price. They did. But how I enjoyed it for that year!

On an evening in July, Hank Senff showed

up at our door, shaking and very wet.

"Hank! What's wrong? What happened?" we asked. "We thought you were in Tanganyika. Are you all right?"

"I'm not too good at the moment." He shivered. "It was a near thing, believe me."

He went on to explain how he had been sitting by the river, waiting for the water to subside so he could cross the Irish bridge.

"When I thought the water was no higher than my waist, I decided to try driving my truck across. I wanted to be done with the crossing before dark so I wasn't stuck on the river bank all night. Everything went well until I made the mistake of stopping midstream to take a picture. Suddenly the truck began to move sideways, caught in the current."

Dallas and I looked at each other. The normally empty rivers were anything but gentle when swollen from the heavy rains. If the currents could sweep Hank's truck away, we shuddered at what they could do to Hank.

"How did you ever escape?" we asked.

"I was climbing out the window, ready to jump and swim for it, when the truck stopped drifting. I was able to drive to shore." He brushed at his thinning hair with shaking hands. "It was a very close thing."

As we sat comforting Hank, across the compound Uncle John and Aunt Mabel's house was being robbed of sheets, towels, blankets, two suitcases and some books. We discovered the theft the next morning when we found some sheets on the ground outside the house.

We called the chief of the village, and he began an investigation straight out of Sherlock Holmes.

"Where are Bwana and Madame Buyse?" he asked.

"In Congo for a visit," we said.

He walked around the house with us and discovered footprints in the mud beneath a window.

"It's a good thing it's rainy season," he said. "Most of the year, no prints."

Taking a long blade of grass, he carefully measured the footprint. Then he had every man in the village come forward to have his foot measured with the blade of grass.

The giant mango tree outside our house was the setting for this procedure. Quietly, one man after another had his foot measured. Suddenly one drunken man refused.

"Slap him sober," the chief told his lieutenants, all too familiar with the man's general troublemaking.

I recognized the disruptive man as someone who had given us problems, too. Once he had walked by the window where I was working and threatened me with the spears in his hand. He had also chased Dallas's national evangelists out of the village when they went there to preach.

The man broke away from the council under

the tree and disappeared into the tall grass before anyone could grab him.

"Don't worry," the chief assured Dallas. "We will catch him."

As Dallas and the chief talked, the belligerent man returned, armed with six spears. All the village men who had gathered to watch the proceedings melted into the grass, neglecting to warn Dallas and the chief. The man crept up behind the two unwary men.

Suddenly he ran at Dallas, swearing and threatening. He pulled one of his spears and hurled it directly at Dallas.

Dallas had put a tree between himself and the man as soon as the attack began. As the spear whizzed past Dallas's thigh, the tree protected him from injury.

When the man threw the spear the men of the village, appalled at the attack, rushed out of the grass, grabbed him and tied him hand and foot. Dallas drove him to the local jail.

"He will get two-and-a-half to five years in jail for this," the chief assured Dallas. "What he did was very wrong. And I tell you, Opari is the worst village in my whole territory."

Of course his assessment of our village didn't help our shaky nerves.

Interestingly, the attacker was not the one who broke into Uncle John and Aunt Mabel's house. The chief found the thieves to be Aunt Mabel's houseboy, a medical boy of Olive's whom I had previously fired and a local workman.

This incident of the attack on Dallas, meant for evil, caused a different attitude to develop among the people. They seemed more receptive to us and the gospel.

"God was with you," they told us, clearly impressed with Dallas' survival.

"Well, let me tell you more about this God who took care of me," Dallas said. And they listened more carefully than ever before.

One Sunday, eight came forward in response to an invitation to trust Jesus as their Savior. Among these eight were old men, something previously unheard of. In a very short time, 73 enrolled in classes to learn more about Jesus.

From our prayer letter, August 1954:

With David of old we can say, "Thou comest to me . . . with a spear, . . . but I come to thee in the name of the LORD of hosts, . . . whom thou hast defied. This day will the LORD deliver thee into my hand" (1 Samuel 17:45-46).

Although this may be true, it can be dangerous. Some have written to us saying they have felt constrained to pray for us a little harder. We praise God for this. All we can say is that when you feel like praying—PRAY!

CHAPTER 13

Missionary Emergencies

In July 1954, the British turned over the government of Sudan to the Sudanese people, making it the first African country to embrace home rule. The anti-British feelings that swept the country affected us and we wondered how long whites would be able to remain.

The south Sudanese were not educated enough to take over the British-vacated positions, so the Arabs of north Sudan filled the jobs. The south Sudanese seemed to prefer the white government to the northern Arabs. They also seemed to prefer their primitive ways to the more sophisticated ways of the Arabs and they resisted all attempts to force change.

A further disruption was the decision of the new Sudanese government to double the wages of the people overnight. We had always had trouble paying our boys on our small missionary support. Now costs were prohibitive.

Consequently Dallas was without much of his help and I was without a cook or hospital boy.

I would start mixing bread at 6:30 each morning. While it rose, I would run up the hill to the dispensary, about two blocks away, and see some patients. Then I'd rush down to shape the bread and set it to rise again. Back up the hill I'd go to give medicine and see more patients. Then down the hill to put the bread in the wood stove. Up the hill for more patients. Down the hill to rescue the bread before it burned. Is it any wonder I was worn out each night?

Dallas built the kids a playhouse. It was only four poles supporting a grass roof, but they loved it and played under it for hours.

Carolyn loved playing with her dolls, toy dishes and pictures of food. She fed everything to her baby, even pork chops which she somehow remembered from the States. Her hair was straight and turning darker all the time.

Kennie played cars and trucks all day and kept running into ditches like Uncle John.

Kay poured cup after cup of "cuffie" and drank them all herself. At two, her hair was still white. She was a tease and showoff and on her second birthday sang, "Happy birthday to me" all day.

By the end of the year my mother guessed I was pregnant again and we announced to our missionary friends that I was five months along, due at the beginning of May.

"It's going to be a boy," Dallas said.

"How do you know that?" I asked.

"I just do," he said. "You'll see."

What I saw for the present was a rash of missionary illnesses. Aunt Mabel became ill, and I couldn't leave her even to go to town.

Then Bill Beatty was stung by a scorpion. A boy traveled 25 miles by bicycle to tell me, and Dallas drove me to Bill. I had to inject the specific medication directly into the already excruciating wound.

In December, Dan Olsen contracted infectious hepatitis, turning chartreuse before they were able to bring him to me at Opari for treatment. They stayed a week, adding a special diet for Dan to our regular planning.

And just at Christmas Aunt Mabel became ill again. My diagnosis, strep throat.

Still we celebrated Christmas; with a feathery tree that wilted an hour after we cut it. We kept it up for several days anyway. Two days after the holiday we drove to Katire Ayom for our Christmas dinner. Dorothy Beatty had brought a turkey back from Congo and kept him alive until this special dinner. We had turkey dressing, mashed potatoes, precious canned corn, peas and ice cream which tasted like home.

We had drawn names, and every adult received a gift. We all gave to the children.

Kennie opened a gift that had been sent to him from home. I could see uncertainty on his face.

"What's this, Mom?" he asked, holding it out.

"It's a telephone," I said. "You talk to people on it."

He looked from me to the phone clearly doubting the wisdom of my answer. He had been too young when we left the States to remember what telephones were and certainly he'd never seen one in Africa.

By the end of our day together, Bill Beatty was down with malaria, and we had to leave sooner than expected. The next day Dallas had to make Bill's planned trip to Torit. How dependent we were on each other. If one of us was ill, the others had to fill in. A station in Sudan usually had three or four adults, never more than five, and we were intricately involved in each other's lives.

Also extremely ill at this time were the Reitsmas at Logotok. Kim, who was expecting in February, had severe bouts of malaria and weeks of bacillary dysentery and scarlet fever. Susie, now five-and-a-half, had scarlet fever twice, pneumonia, dysentery and malaria and almost died three times. Dr. Doug had dysentery and cerebral malaria with attendant convulsions. Year-old Jessie also had scarlet fever and dysentery.

Barbara Battye cared for the ill Reitsma children until she came down with scarlet fever and dysentery too.

Finally the Reitsmas acknowledged that they couldn't remain in Logotok but needed further treatment, especially Doug. They had been hoping that the new baby could be born at the station, but they allowed Hank Senff to drive them to Oicha, Congo, for proper care.

A week after the Reitsmas left, their home and hospital were burned to the ground. They lost everything, thousands of dollars worth of medical supplies as well as all their personal things.

"Everything?" we asked when we heard the news.

"Everything," we were told.

"That's the house we stayed in when we first came to Sudan," I said.

"It's gone," we were told. "And only Barbara was on the station when it happened."

"Is she all right?"

"Fine. It's been determined it was set by men from another village who had been feuding with the Latukas. The Latukas would be injured fighting this tribe, come to Doug's dispensary for treatment and return to the fight after they were fixed up. The arsonists figured that if they got rid of the dispensary, then the men wouldn't return to the fight and they might win."

All my correspondence to Mom was now full of the usual requests for clothes, nutmeg, sugar, black pepper, canning lids, a glass top for a percolator and orders for Montgomery Ward through her to save time. They were also full of lists of baby needs. She and the ladies of her

Sunday School class and the folks at the Long Branch church were ever faithful.

The Long Branch church raised $400 and bought me surgical equipment, obstetrical forceps, an otoscope, a 21-quart pressure cooker (for use in canning and as an autoclave) and other instruments to use at the dispensary. I felt very professional with these things in spite of my extremely primitive working conditions. We had to pay $110 to get these supplies through customs. There were many discouragements during these months. Rome was wooing the Sudanese government. Islam had leaped from North Africa to South Africa, seeking to engulf the whole continent. There was great unrest among leaders who had been steady for years. Young men, at each station, who said they had trusted Christ as Savior, went their own ways, turning their backs on Christ. Would Christ's Church ever be established among these tribes we wondered?

"Why," Mom wrote about this time, "are you planning to go 250 miles to Rethy, Congo, to have the baby? Isn't Logotok and Dr. Reitsma a lot closer?"

"Yes," I answered. "Closer in distance. But the 105 miles of road to Logotok are so horrendous that the 250 miles to Rethy is quicker and kinder to car and passenger. Also, Rethy has a hospital, equipment and a guest house for the family while I will be occupied."

On April 7, we left for Rethy and the birth of

our fourth child. We drove all the way in one day without mishap, my emergency delivery kit of two clamps, scissors and cord resting on the seat between us—just in case. As we drove into the yard of the guest house, the car collapsed on its wheels. What gracious keeping by the hand of God.

At Rethy we lived in a four-room furnished brick house with electricity for several hours each evening. What luxury! There was the cooler weather to enjoy and the plentiful supply of vegetables. I canned 35 pints to take home. I also did all the washing and ironing, hoping to hurry the baby along. Once I even got to use a washing machine!

We waited at Rethy for three weeks. By April 27, I was anxious to get things over with and Dr. Barnett was anxious to go away. He ordered castor oil to step up the few pains I was having. An hour later, the pains were very strong and we sent the kids "boarding" to the other missionary families.

We were none too soon because suddenly I started passing large clots of blood.

"Placenta previa," said the doctor, then explained for Dallas, "The placenta is separating from the wall of the uterus prematurely, before the baby is born. Wrong order."

He put me in bed in the guest house where we were staying. My contractions were two minutes apart for five hours.

Dr. Barnett went to the hospital to scrub.

Dallas took me in the car as close to the door of the hospital as possible even driving one block over very bumpy lawn. All this time, I was pushing.

Dallas stopped, and between pains, I literally ran into the hospital, ran down the hall and jumped onto the delivery table. Dr. Barnett stepped into place just in time to catch the baby's head.

Dallas was with me, his first time to witness the birth of one of his children. It made quite an impression on him and his prayer of thanksgiving at my side was one of our special times.

"Lord," Dallas prayed, quoting from First Samuel, "we have lent him to You for as long as he shall live."

One benefit of Dallas's presence at our son's delivery was that I got to choose the baby's name. We had been debating about it.

"After all you've been through, you deserve to call him what ever you want to," my husband said.

Birth Certificate:
(In French and 24 inches long)

RETHY HOSPITAL
Rethy, Congo Belge, Africa
April 28, 1955
TO WHOM IT MAY CONCERN:
This is to state that I attended the birth of
a son: JEFFREY CARLTON GREEN

Born: April 27, 1955, 8:50 P.M. (Wed.)
Weight: 7 pounds, 8 ounces
Father: Dallas S. Green
Mother: Winifred Grace Gordon Green
Residence: Africa Inland Mission, Torit, Sudan
Parents' Nationality: American, U.S.A. citizens
Witness: Dr. Arthur Barnett

CHAPTER 14

Escape from Logotok

Carolyn was delighted with her new brother and enjoyed playing little mother. She was a great help with Kennie and Kay too.

Kennie seemed mostly indifferent toward Carlie's arrival. "But I'm glad we got another boy so Daddy and me aren't the only ones. Now we're even."

Kay wasn't too sure about this little competitor for my attention. She would stand beside me and cry for me to hold her instead of him.

America or Africa, I thought. *It doesn't matter. Kids are kids.*

As it turned out, the main disruption in our family came not from Carl's arrival but from yet another move. As soon as we returned from Rethy, we were asked to relocate to Logotok in another game of missionary shuffle. Scheduled and completed furloughs prompted the latest shift in personnel.

Not again! I thought, dreading the work involved. *Though, God, Logotok is the place to which*

You originally called us to serve and the Latukas are the people You called us to reach.

By the time of the actual move I was even excited that we would be giving the gospel to people who had never had a chance to respond to the claims of Jesus. By this time, the people at Opari had heard many times and mostly hardened their hearts, a very discouraging thing. We had such hopes after Dallas had the run-in with the spear-throwing man. The people had responded to us and the church so well—for a short time.

So we went to Logotok and I took Dr. Doug Reitsma's place as he and his family went to the States for a much-needed furlough. Dallas served as Logotok station superintendent.

When we had lived there two years before, Kay had been a baby and the Latuka women had been amused and appalled at Dallas's involvement in her care. Now we were back with another baby and again the women laughed at us, especially when I tried to tell them that Dallas could feed Carl. How strange we Americans were to them!

One day I took the coat I had made for Carolyn when she was three and tried it on Kay. She looked adorable and we took her picture because it was surely the only time she'd ever wear the garment.

The houseboys laughed and laughed at the strange outfit. They couldn't begin to comprehend a degree of cold that would require protection of that magnitude.

Carlie, after a rocky start that required formula to supplement his nursing, was doing very well. He had a double chin, a darling smile and he was the only one of our kids not born bald. I put a mirror on his changing table, and he talked to it as I changed him. He would look at me in the mirror with his large, dark eyes, turn and look at the real me, and coo and laugh.

I had picked up a battered baby carriage in Congo, purchased some heavy green plastic and covered the frame for a rolling bed for Carlie. It was a lot of work, but I was proud of the finished product.

The Africans were impressed with me at how expert I was at the art of "borning."

"Girl, boy, girl, boy is good," they told us. "You sell the first girl for cows and goats which you use to buy a wife for the boy. Then you sell the other girl and buy a wife for the other boy."

At least there was something in our family patterns they approved of.

This time in Logotok we were able to purchase milk from the Latukas. Previously they had always insisted on adulterating their milk with cow's urine, first by washing the udders with urine before milking, then by adding urine to the milk itself.

Finally we persuaded them to keep ours untreated. I smelled each container they brought me before I bought it. Of course, we still boiled the milk thoroughly before use.

We had a picnic to celebrate the Fourth of July. We even butchered a cow and had hamburgers on homemade buns, a real treat. When we told the houseboys we were celebrating a holiday, they laughed at us again. When we told them that no one went to work or school on this day, they really laughed. It was one more proof that we were very strange indeed.

About this time, a little girl of 12 came to the dispensary with two crushed fingers. I was able to save one finger but not the other. I had to amputate without anesthetic. Poor child.

A man was brought in, mauled by a lion. I don't know how he survived. Crucial bleeding points in his groin, neck and temple were severed. A fraction of an inch was all that prevented him from bleeding to death. I cleaned the wounds, sewed them up and gave him sulfa and penicillin. Because the man was a chief, a retinue of 20 or so watched the whole procedure.

The next day 30 extra people came to church with him. They wanted to watch me dress the wounds after church and they knew we didn't give medicine unless the patient went to church. Consequently we had our largest congregation ever, about 65.

A woman was carried in from a village about 10 miles away. She had a baby the day before, but the placenta had not delivered. I removed it manually, hoping I got it all. How I longed for a doctor! But the Africans were satisfied with attention and an injection. To them, needles did it all.

If I tried to give them oral medicine for a specific treatment, they'd say, "Oh, no, Madame. No *dawa*. I want a needle. I'll even pay you more if you'll give me a needle."

Since they were paying the equivalent of 25 cents a year for health care, I wasn't swayed by the great financial rewards of injections though I often gave them.

Dallas built a dispensary to replace Doug Reitsma's that had been burned down. He took an abandoned native stone hut, 15 by 15 with six-foot walls. He built the walls higher with bricks and put a metal roof on it so we would have a more secure place to store medical supplies.

As the weeks passed, the tensions between north Sudan and south Sudan increased. The north controlled the communication system and censored the news the outside world received. The north, wanting no help or interference from anyone, were convinced they could run the country well themselves. They even took over the telegraph office in Torit to curtail southern contact with the outside. The south, by contrast, wanted to appeal to the United States for help but were largely unable to do so because of communications limitations.

Then came Friday, August 19, 1955, the day of the unending drums, the day the south rebelled against the north.

"Don't go to Torit, Dallas," came the word over the radio, but Dallas and Kennie were already a day into their trip to Juba, a trip that required them to drive through Torit each way.

Barb and I, fearful of what might happen if we stayed alone where we were, packed up and left Logotok. Hearts pounding, palms sweating, we drove toward Torit, hoping to intercept Dallas along the way, hoping for help from fellow missionary Sid Langford.

"We'll probably meet Daddy on the road, coming back for us," Barb and I told the kids. "Don't worry. We'll see him and Kennie soon."

But Dallas didn't come, Torit was in a state of anarchy and Sid's house was empty.

"It's too dangerous to go to Juba," Barb said. "If there's fighting, it's in that direction."

Dallas's direction. Kennie's direction.

I nodded. "South is our only choice. And we can stop at Katire Ayom on the way. Maybe the Beattys will have a better idea what's going on than we do."

We had already been on the road most of the day, passing countless warriors standing by the road, spears and sometimes guns in hand, waving our white arms so they would know we weren't the northern enemy. The warriors were as uncertain and nervous as we were and knew no more about what was going on than we did.

Now into the night we drove, too exhausted

to be hungry. The girls huddled in the back-seat, quiet and well-behaved, probably because they caught our tension. Carlie nestled peacefully in my arms.

Dear God, I'm scared—but I'm not. I don't know what's going to happen, but You do, and that's enough for me. Go before us, and keep us safe. And take care of Dallas and Kennie, too. Please.

Just before the Katire Ayom turn-off we came to a river that needed to be forded on irregular slabs of rock. Even when Dallas and I traveled in the daytime, we had a boy walk ahead of the vehicle to show the extremely narrow safe path through the water.

"I don't know if I can do this," Barb said as we listened to the great rush of rain-swollen water, such a loud sound in the dark.

"Sure you can," I said, wondering myself.

She shook her head. "If we slide off the rocks into the water, we'll be stuck in more than one way. We might even get swept along by the current." Her hands were clenched on the steering wheel and her face pinched with fatigue. "I can't do it. I really can't."

We stared at the turbulent water. I knew I certainly couldn't drive across.

"If only it weren't rainy season," I muttered.

Taking a deep breath, I climbed out of the car.

"Here, Carolyn. Hold Carlie," I said, putting the baby in her arms.

"What are you doing, Winifred?" Barb asked.

I pulled off my shoes. "I'm going wading."

"Dear Jesus," Carolyn immediately prayed. "Keep Mommy safe." Every time we had gotten stuck on the road, she'd prayed that we'd get unstuck, and when we did, she never failed to thank Jesus for helping us. I smiled at her and Kay and Carl. What great kids!

Trying not to think about all the diseases lurking in the dark, unfriendly water and the jagged stones waiting to cut my feet and give the germs access, I waded across the river, my shoes held high above my head. The tug of the current was amazingly strong. I kept trying not to think of Hank and his almost-swept-away truck.

After forever, I reached the other side and walked toward the nearest village, hoping against hope for word about the missionaries at Katire.

"I'm sorry, Madame," I was told. "The missionaries left this morning, and they haven't returned."

For once I was glad the Africans were so fascinated with us that they noted everything we did. I hiked disconsolately back to Barb and the kids with the sad news.

"Dear Jesus," prayed Carolyn. "Thank You for keeping Mommy safe."

With flashlight in hand, I walked ahead of the van leading the way over the rocks. Barb had the extra strength to keep going

We continued driving south, farther away

from Dallas and Kennie and toward Uganda. We had not gone far when a vehicle approached us, blinking its lights at us, then spotlighting us.

We stopped and a whole company of soldiers fanned out in the darkness.

"The signal!" one screamed at us. "What's the signal?"

Barb and I looked at each other. How were we supposed to know any signal? Heart hammering, I waved my hand frantically out the window.

Suddenly an officer jumped onto our running board.

"Oh, Madame!" he shouted, clearly agitated. "I had my gun aimed at you, ready to shoot. Then you waved and I saw your white skin. Oh, Madame! I almost killed you!"

Trying to act like my heart wasn't pounding and my throat wasn't dry with fear, I greeted him. "We're trying to get the children to safety," I explained.

"Where's Bwana?" he asked.

"He's away on a trip," I said.

"But it's not safe for you women to be alone on the road on this night!"

I agreed wholeheartedly.

"I will fix the problem," he said. "Two of my men will escort you."

He gave an order, and two soldiers jumped onto our running board and rode with us as we started on our way again.

Very shortly another truck approached.

"It's an army truck," one of the guards said, and I was extremely glad for our armed companions.

As the truck got closer and our headlights illuminated the grill, I realized it wasn't an army truck at all.

"It's Sid and Bill!" I cried.

Both vehicles stopped, everyone climbed out and we had a little praise service right there in the middle of the road.

"We've just taken the rest of our missionaries to Uganda," Sid said. "We're on our way back for you folks."

"You haven't by some miracle seen Dallas and Kennie, have you?" I asked.

The two men shook their heads, not surprising since they had been driving south and Dallas had gone toward Juba, but it was disappointing nonetheless.

"Come on back to Katire for the night," Bill said. "You're exhausted."

And we were, though neither Barb nor I slept much after we fell into bed. We kept "driving" the van in our sleep.

The next day Bill said, "Sort through your luggage, Winifred. Take only what's absolutely necessary."

I weeded out expendables and Bill packed our things in the back of his pickup.

"Winifred, you've brought kerosene with you. What do you plan to do with that?"

"No," I said. "I brought gasoline."

He held up a container, and sure enough, in the rush to leave Logotok, I had brought kerosene instead of gasoline.

"Oh, Bill! What if we had refueled!" I shivered at the thought of being stuck who knew where because I had made such a terrible mistake.

"Don't worry," Bill said. "Nothing happened."

Once again the good hand of God was obviously upon us.

Bill drove us to Uganda to join his family and the other missionaries. We would wait to see what happened politically in Sudan before we returned.

"How were you able to get enough gas to do all this driving?" I asked Bill, crammed with Barb and the kids into the cab of his truck.

"It's funny," Bill said. "I was coming back from getting the kids at school, and I felt the Lord nudge me to buy two extra drums of gas. I did, never realizing how they would be needed."

After seven grueling hours with little food or water, we finally reached the safety of the Ugandan border. Enroute, we asked everyone we passed about Dallas and Kennie. No one had seen them.

Oh, Lord, please keep them safe. Please let us find each other soon!

I spent the night with British missionaries in

Gulu, Uganda, frightened and bone weary. My arms ached from holding Carlie for two solid days and from waving at people all along the way so they could see my white skin. My back pain was excruciating. I was worried about our home and the dispensary. I had no idea where my husband and son were or if they were dead or alive. I was undoubtedly not the most congenial guest these dear people had ever had but they were lovely to us.

At 9 o'clock the next morning, a Sunday, Bill returned to Katire to join Sid who had stayed behind to protect mission property. The rest of us, 19 in all, squeezed ourselves and our baggage into two station wagons. I was amazed at the "necessary" things I was able to again prune from our luggage, including a large basket of dirty clothes and wet diapers.

The kids and I drove to Rethy in a station wagon stuffed with Dan and Jean Olsen, Dorothy Beatty and her three kids and Barb, plus our luggage. Jennie Langford drove the other station wagon loaded with her four kids, Aunt Mabel, Olive Rawn, Betty Wilson and their luggage.

We ran out of water part way to Rethy, and everyone was thirsty. Three miles from Rethy our car also ran out of gas. Jennie's car went on and sent folks back to help us.

How wonderful dinner tasted and bed felt that night! All told we had traveled 400 miles from Logotok, 400 miles of anxiety, discomfort and stress, but we could do nothing except thank the Lord for His hand of protection on all of us.

"Dear Jesus," prayed Carolyn as I put her down for the night, "thank You for keeping us safe. And be with Daddy and Kennie. Keep them safe from the bad men."

Amen. Amen and amen.

Rethy Academy had just closed for vacation, so we were housed in the dorms. Again God's hand was visible in the timing of everything, for where else could such a large group be cared for? I was kept busy washing clothes and caring for the kids. It was good to be occupied so I didn't have too much time to think about Dallas and Kennie. And Carolyn and Kay had a wonderful time with the Langford and Beatty children. They hadn't had playmates like this in months.

Dallas and Kennie had been gone a week and a day before I had any word of them. Then came a radio message from Aba, Congo.

"We've received a cable, Winifred," I was told. "Dallas and Kennie are safe! They're in Khartoum."

"Khartoum?" I was stunned. The one place I had not dreamed they would be was in the capital of Sudan, 1,000 miles north.

"When will they get here?" I asked. Now that I knew they were safe, all I wanted was to see them, to hug them.

"No word on that," I was told.

So I waited some more, but at least I now waited without fear.

Word about this civil war did not reach the U.S. media until sometime later. Since mail took three to four weeks to reach the States our families were not aware of our plight until weeks after our evacuation.

Letter to Mom, September 2, 1955:

We have been taking things comparatively easy here at Rethy. We women spend a few hours cooking and cleaning up, washing and ironing, but there is time to sit around and read. We do not have the vaguest idea when we will return to Sudan, or if we will. Fighting is still going on, though a truce is supposed to be in effect. We are all fine. The children are doing well in this lovely climate with all the wonderful fruits and vegetables. Carlie is a little darling and growing well.

CHAPTER 15

Caught in the Crossfire

"Mommy!" Kennie came flying toward me. I wrapped my arms around him, then around his father. I cried so hard I could barely talk. Carolyn and Kay hugged everyone happily.

"Oh, I'm so glad to see you!" I sobbed into Dallas's neck.

"No more than I to see you, honey," Dallas said. "Two weeks and two days is forever!"

After everyone at Rethy welcomed Dallas and Kennie home, still wearing the same clothes they had been wearing when they left, we sat back to hear their story.

"Well," said Dallas, "you know we left Thursday morning, the 18th, for Juba, taking Ohide, our boy, with us. We got to Torit about 6:15 in the morning, picked up the mail for Opari, Katire Ayom and us, and left about 7:00. The stores hadn't opened yet and everything appeared normal to me.

"Halfway to Juba we had a flat tire and it took about an hour to fix it. Several trucks passed us heading for Torit, but I didn't think anything of the heavy traffic."

"The first northern troops?" I asked.

Dallas nodded. "I think so. It must have been about this time that the fighting in Torit began."

So close, I thought. I hugged Kennie tighter as he sat beside me.

"After fixing a second flat about seven miles from the Juba ferry, we arrived at the Nile about 11:45. The ferry was tied up on the far side. The people who were wandering around waiting told us the ferry had stopped running because two men were shot on the Juba side of the river.

"Couldn't you just have come home then?" I asked.

"I didn't have enough gas," Dallas said. "So Kennie, Ohide and I settled down to wait."

"I had some crackers," said Kennie. "And then the soldiers came and set up their machine guns. They pointed them at us."

I hoped Kennie couldn't see how upset I was at this news, but Dallas could.

"Well, not at *us*," he said quickly. "The soldiers were on the Juba side of the river and they pointed the guns across at our side."

I sagged with relief and Kennie said, "Don't squeeze me so hard, Mommy."

"About 4 o'clock," Dallas continued, "the ferry crossed the river with six soldiers aboard. They told Kennie and me and a man from Uganda to get on board, but we had to leave our vehicles."

"They wouldn't let Ohide come with us," Kennie said. "We had to leave him. All he had to eat was some peanuts."

"When we got to Juba," said Dallas, "we went to the hotel. We were no sooner there than a sound truck went through the streets announcing martial law and a curfew after dark."

"They shot some guns, Mommy," said Kennie. "They shot at the hotel."

I looked at Dallas, and he nodded. "Over the hotel really, with answering shots from the governor's office across the street. I don't know what happened in terms of anyone getting hurt. We couldn't go see because it was getting dark already. I don't think we slept too well, did we, Kennie?"

"Too many trucks driving around," Kennie said.

"The next day, the city was like a ghost town. All the stores and the market were closed and police stood everywhere, bristling with rifles and ammunition. We walked to the mission bookstore a couple of blocks from the hotel and borrowed a car to get gas. I decided that the best plan was to go to the ferry and try to get back across the river. Then we'd go to Opari. I managed to get 10 gallons of gas. I think it was Kennie's presence."

Kennie smiled with importance.

"We were at the ferry by 10:00 a.m.," Dallas continued. " 'You have to have papers to cross,' the lieutenant in charge said. 'From the governor and written in Arabic.' So we went to the Commandant of Police and asked him the procedure to get the papers from the governor. 'I can get that for you,' he said. And he called the governor's office. 'Tell them they can go,' the governor said. So we went back to the ferry. 'No papers, no crossing,' the lieutenant said. Back to the police station. 'We've just had a call from the governor's office,' the Commandant said. 'It's no longer safe to cross the river. They expect fighting any minute.' "

"So you were trying to get out of Juba while Barb and I were trying to get to Torit to find you," I said.

Dallas nodded. "And we kept trying. By now the roads were all blocked and the airport was closed to civilian traffic. All planes were flying northern troops into Juba to put down what they saw as the southern rebellion. As the planes landed and the soldiers disembarked, families of the northern Sudanese living in Juba crowded on to be flown to Khartoum and safety.

"The officials said that if all was quiet during the night, maybe Kennie and I could leave Saturday. It must not have been quiet because we weren't allowed to leave. On Sunday all foreigners were told to be ready to leave at an hour's notice."

"Then a car came for us, Mommy," said Kenny. "It took us to the ferry."

"They wanted our truck in Juba for 'safe-keeping'," Dallas explained.

"I take it you haven't seen the truck since it went into 'safe-keeping'?" How strong and solid my husband looked, sitting there with a daughter on each knee.

Dallas nodded. "And we had to leave Ohide a second time. Poor man. By this time we were hearing all sorts of rumors of atrocities. Kennie and I went to stay with Archdeacon Gibson, a British missionary. The archdeacon had been on safari when the trouble broke out and he had come through 24 barricades to get home. The Africans let him through because they recognized him and knew of his years of service to them. He told us about killing and burning and looting. He saw many villages in shambles with the northern Sudanese killed by the rebels."

"I didn't like them hurting each other, Mommy," said Kennie, his voice shaky. "I missed you. And we had to wash our clothes every night. I washed the socks."

"Kennie was wonderful," said Dallas. "He was brave and very, very good."

Kennie straightened a bit, proud of his father's compliments.

"On Monday, August 22," said Dallas, "the

new Sudanese Prime Minister sent a surrender order down from Khartoum. The southern rebels in Torit refused to obey it, so the north laid plans to attack Torit as soon as armored cars could arrive from Khartoum, a somewhat lengthy process of two weeks. Meanwhile the news was so incomplete and fuzzy."

"The north doesn't like the idea of such trouble so early into self-determination," I said. "Makes them look bad in the eyes of the world."

"Your southern prejudices are showing," said Dallas with a smile.

"Well, they are our people," I said. "And they took good care of the kids and Barb and me."

Dallas nodded. "I agree. But there we were in northern hands, being treated quite well, too. 'We'll send you north to Khartoum,' they told us on Monday. 'No, please. We want to go south to Congo and our family.' 'North,' they said. 'There is no safe way to go south.' So inside an hour Kennie and I were flying to Khartoum.

"When we landed, I called the Sudan Interior Mission. I couldn't believe it when Hank Senff answered. He came and picked us up, and we stayed with the SIM missionaries."

"I went to kindergarten, Mommy!" Kennie's voice sang. Clearly this was one part of his adventure he had enjoyed. "I went with all the kids. Then I got sick."

"Oh, Kennie," I said. "Again? I'm so sorry."

"It's OK. It was only Thursday and Friday. I took my medicine and got better. Then Daddy took me to the zoo and I fed peanuts to the animals."

"You had all kinds of adventures, kiddo," I said. "But I'm glad you're back with me. I'm glad we're all back with each other."

"Me, too." And Kennie snuggled closer.

"It was no easy job, getting us here," Dallas said. "I called on all the officials in Khartoum and none of them could or would help. Then I tried to find a way out apart from the government. Sobelair, which flew near Rethy, didn't have a seat available until October 14! Sabina didn't have air rights to land in Khartoum. BOAC flew out of Khartoum but went way south in Uganda to Entebbe.

"By this time, I was out of money. I had landed in Khartoum with only four pounds (about $12). When I got word to report to the airport at 2:45 a.m. Monday for a possible flight out of Khartoum, SIM gave me two blank checks to pay for the tickets, one for actual use and the second in case there was an error of some kind in the writing and I needed to make out another.

"Kennie and I went through customs and immigration. I got some coffee and we settled down to wait. At dawn we got word that our plane would not be taking us after all. We turned in our tickets and tore up the first check just as a BOAC plane landed. While it was refueling and the passengers were resting in the lounge I asked where the plane was going. Entebbe, I was told. I asked if they had seats for Kennie and me and they said yes! Just 10 minutes before the plane took off I wrote the second check and we boarded.

"We got to Entebbe early afternoon and went to the hotel. It had a beautiful view of Lake Victoria, free swimming, golfing, tennis and excellent food and coffee."

"So you two are in luxury while we're here washing laundry, crammed into the dorm, huh?" I teased.

"Well, honey, we couldn't enjoy the facilities because we were missing you so much," Dallas said with a smile. "Besides we weren't there long enough to do anything. I was preparing to book a flight to Congo when I saw a fellow missionary who had come to pick up other missionaries returning from furlough and take them to Congo. When they offered us a ride, we jumped at the opportunity. And here we are!"

From Dallas' letter, September 1955:

How thankful we were for all God had done for us during our time of separation from our loved ones and fellow-workers. After we made it to Entebbe, Uganda, a missionary friend invited us to return to Congo with him. We accepted with great pleasure, realizing God's providential leading in this meeting.

We journeyed with him to the Congo border, where we met another missionary who was going to Rethy. By Saturday afternoon we rejoiced together in the goodness of the Lord who had reunited our family.

CHAPTER 16

Mommie, The Nurse Is Ill

On September 19, one month after our flight, we headed back to Logotok, Barb Battye traveling with us.

News about the actual situation in south Sudan was sketchy because communications were so poor. We had heard that over 400 northerners were killed in the rebellion and so were an unknown number of southerners; the number being uncertain because so many had disappeared into the bush. The south now had an army of occupation in residence.

There was still no mail service to or from Torit because the postmaster had been killed and the post office looted. Logotok, Opari and Katire Ayom, our three mission stations, were completely cut off from the world and things were tense and unpredictable.

But Dallas and I agreed: We should go home. We drove from Rethy to Gulu, Uganda, so

163

we could pick up the "necessities" I had left behind on our flight. There they were, the dirty diapers and damp clothes still in the basket just as I had left them, only now they were mildewed.

We stayed in Gulu overnight, and in the morning when I bent over the wash basin, to my horror, I couldn't straighten up.

Lord, not my back on top of everything else! And so far from home!

Carefully Dallas bundled me into the car, packing me in like a fragile treasure. To his dismay no position was pain-free and I gasped as the spasms knifed. I was thankful for the British missionary who gave me some strong pain medicine and a hot water bottle.

When we got to Opari, I could go no farther. The pain had escalated beyond agonizing to excruciating, much aggravated by the rough roads. Dallas left me, Barb and the kids with Aunt Mabel and went on to Katire to get Olive Rawn to nurse me. She brought pain medicine and muscle relaxants with her and while Barb watched the three older kids, Olive cared for Carlie and me.

Dallas left again, this time to go to Logotok to check on things there. Eight miles out of Opari the fuel pump failed.

"I had to send a boy to get Uncle John to come for me," he told us. "And the frustrating thing is that I've a new fuel pump at Logotok!"

Often during this time Dallas and I would

look at each other and wonder what was happening to our missionary work. All we seemed to encounter were complications and delays, illness and uncertainty.

"I know God's guiding," I'd say around my pain.

"I know it, too," Dallas would say through his frustration.

But we didn't understand.

We set up housekeeping in Aunt Mabel's tiny two-room guest house. One room was bedroom/dining room, the other kitchen/pantry/closet/washroom. The "little house" was up the path, farther than was comfortable from our guest house.

My back treatment consisted mostly of sitting in a tub of hot water, trying to soak out the soreness and tension. This meant that gallons of water had to be hauled from the well, heated over an open fire and poured in and out of the galvanized metal tub. I felt so terrible causing all that work for everyone!

And on top of everything else, I had a very bad siege of malaria.

After a few days Olive said, "I've got to go back to Katire."

My heart sank, but I knew she was right. Bill Beatty was there, sicker than I and needing her nursing skills more. He had almost died three times and he had to be fed intravenously and catheterized. Plans were being made to transport him to Congo.

"If my car was working," said Dallas, "I'd take him. But I still don't have a fuel pump."

In the middle of these emergencies, Kennie spiked a high temperature. When we gave him extra aralen as a guard against malaria, he went to sleep. He woke and began to convulse, was unconscious for an hour, cried for a half hour until he slept again, then twitched for four hours.

Kay had already kept us awake the previous night coughing and vomiting, so we started her on aralen, too. Next Carolyn came down with the same symptoms.

I had no idea what I would do if Dallas ever became sick.

At 2:00 a.m. Tuesday, October 11, Sid and Jennie Langford came through, driving two vehicles, taking the Beattys to Dr. Becker. The secret fear was that Bill had polio because he had lost use of his arms and hands.

Jennie drove 36 straight hours with Bill lying on a mattress in the back of her station wagon. Upon arriving at Oicha, Congo, Bill was diagnosed as having malaria with neuritis. Sid arrived the next day with the Beattys' truck, delayed enroute by a motor fire.

Bill was so weak that his recovery was prolonged. Olive Rawn, who had accompanied Bill, the pregnant Dorothy and little Barbie, once again came to the rescue, exercising Bill's arms regularly. After two months of therapy he could raise one hand to his mouth. He never did regain full use of his right arm.

In the middle of all this, Carlie not only had infected ears; he also fell off the bed onto the cement floor. He cried and cried when I touched him, and I diagnosed a broken clavicle. I looked in my first aid book, made a triangular bandage and immobilized the arm. I must have been right, because he was soon well.

Just as I felt well enough for the final phase of the trip back home to Logotok, Barb came down with malaria and was bedridden for a week. Finally, on October 19, we returned to Logotok where the villagers were quite glad to see us. They seemed to feel safer with us present.

We found our storeroom broken into and 15 pounds of Klim, a bag of rock salt and several car springs stolen. This was not surprising since these flat-leaf springs made wonderful axes, hatchets and spears. Many of my home-canned foods had been opened and left to spoil. Our two calves were dead and about 15 of my chickens were gone. We were just glad the house was standing.

Barb's house had been broken into, too. They had rifled through her clothes but not taken any, searched for money, found none and taken some medicine. Barb was most happy when some of her girls came back to help her and learn from her.

The day we arrived was Kay's third birthday. I had no cake mixes and no eggs. I kept watching the few remaining chickens for an egg, but none cooperated. I couldn't even find a village woman to sell me a "good" egg. I always tested their eggs by placing them in a tin of water. If they floated, they were fertilized and would probably contain already growing eyes and other body parts. I only purchased the eggs that didn't float.

Kay's birthday cake was a round, eggless shortcake with pudding between the layers and confectioners sugar sprinkled on top. Three candles burned on top. The kids seemed as pleased as if it were a fancy cake. We gave all three children gifts because Carolyn had missed her birthday and we couldn't slight Kennie.

We had been home only three days when Dallas fell about 10 feet from the bamboo rafters to the floor of our storeroom. He got up easily and we didn't give it another thought. He preached Sunday but by Tuesday he was very hot and couldn't walk.

South Sudan had finally gotten even my husband.

I treated him first for malaria, but after a course of treatment there was no improvement.

Perhaps his trouble was infection from the cuts that he received when he fell. I put him on sulfa and penicillin as well as aralen. He continued to have bad chills and high fevers, hard on a man who had never been sick in his life. I noticed, though, that he only missed one meal.

Finally I sent a runner for Sid and help. It

took me a long time to convince someone to go. The northerners were still in charge of Torit as well as all of Equatoria Province, and our people had a great fear of them. It took my reluctant volunteer 24 hours to ride Dallas's bike the 42 miles to Torit. But what a relief to finally hear Sid pray for Dallas the words of John 11:3: "Lord, . . . he whom thou lovest is sick."

The Swiss-Russian doctor Sid had brought with him confirmed my diagnosis of malaria and gave more quinine. Dallas slowly recovered.

On Wednesday, November 2, we both got up ready to do a full day's work. Dallas was still white and weak but he felt pretty well. Suddenly it was I who was ill as a terrible pain ripped through my right groin. In a half hour I had a fever of 102 and severe chills.

For nearly a week my fever was 102-104 and the chills and sweats were constant. I read my medical books until I couldn't see the words. Then Dallas read them to me. From what I could understand I wasn't long for this world with the type of malaria I diagnosed. In my delirium I heard angel choirs and children singing and knew my end was near.

Dallas decided to take me to Torit for medical care. Carlie would stay at Logotok with Barb and Carolyn would also stay to help. Kennie and Kay would go with us.

Dallas prepared a mattress in the van for me. He and Barb helped me out of bed. When I tried to stand I had such intense pain in my left knee that I collapsed. Dallas and Barb half-carried, half-dragged me to the car. I took some aspirin and some other medicine to make myself sleep. It didn't work, but I was so ill that I barely felt the bumps and ruts as Dallas drove. Everything was hazy and vague and nebulous. The angel choirs sang loudly.

When we got to Torit, the Swiss-Russian doctor was away. We decided to leave the next morning for Aba, Congo, and Dr. Kleinschmidt. During that long, interminable day and night, I existed on frozen orange sections Jennie Langford had in her freezer and on the arthritis medicine Sid's dad had brought along on his visit from the States.

In the morning when Sid and Dallas tried to help me to the car the pain was so agonizing that I fainted. I came to as they were tugging me onto the mattress. I spent the whole trip seeing faces in the clouds and listening to the angelic choirs sing sweetly once more.

When we finally arrived at Aba, Mrs. Kleinschmidt, a nurse, came out to meet us.

"The doctor is in surgery," she said. "But we'll get Winifred settled in the house of a missionary on furlough."

Four African male nurses carried me up the hill and Dallas and Mrs. Kleinschmidt got me to bed. I was absolutely miserable. The medicine had long since worn off and my leg was extremely painful.

Finally Dr. Kleinschmidt was free and gave me a thorough examination. He drew blood for lab analysis and did a spinal tap to check for polio. That really frightened me.

About the only thing I remember of the whole process was the doctor looking at me and asking, "Do you always talk this slowly?"

Dr. Kleinschmidt would not discuss his diagnosis with us from Tuesday until Saturday. Finally he said, "I'm not certain what's wrong with you. Your spinal fluid is clear, but I'm not willing to rule out polio yet."

Part of the reason for his hesitance to rule out polio was that I had developed paralysis in my left leg from hip to knee joint and then all the way to my foot. I was in terrific pain and I was delirious much of the time.

It was policy that the families of patients eased the medical staff's work load by caring for their relatives. Dallas shopped for our food and fed me. Mrs. Kleinschmidt came and bathed me daily. Our family was quarantined until a diagnosis could be made. The kids played quietly outside, helping Dallas as much as they could.

While we were at Aba, we received word that the Olsens were at Rethy for medical treatment. It was incredible. Counting the Beattys who were still at Oicha, three of our key families were off the field due to illness.

By the second week at Aba I could move my leg from side to side. At the end of the second week, I could sit up in a wheel chair for 15 minutes before the pain became unbearable.

As I improved somewhat, I began to miss Carolyn and Carlie desperately. There was no way Dallas could leave me to go get them.

"If it's possible," we radioed, "could Sid bring Carolyn and Carlie the next time he comes this way?"

Even as we sent the message, I doubted Sid would have time for such an errand. We'd just have to wait until I was well enough for Dallas to leave.

Tuesday, November 22, we were both very discouraged when I tried to walk.

"Dallas," I sobbed, "my leg won't move. I just can't make it move!"

"It'll be OK," he comforted, sitting by my bed. "Just relax and try to sleep." And he prayed for me as he frequently did.

He was interrupted by noise outside.

"That sounds like Jennie Langford," I said, struggling to sit up. And suddenly there was Carolyn jumping into Dallas's arms and Jennie carrying Carlie.

"I hardly recognize him," I said as I took the baby. "He's grown so much in just three weeks."

"Look, Mommy!" Carolyn smiled broadly and showed the gap where her front tooth had been. Then she reached in her little purse and took out a shilling. "The tooth fairy came!"

Good old Barb, I thought. *She came through*

when I couldn't. How I appreciated her. And we couldn't thank Jennie and Sid enough. They had heard our message, left for Logotok the same day and gotten the kids. What wonderful friends!

Dallas' work tripled now that the baby was with us and I tried harder than ever to walk, even though I wanted to quit many times because of the pain.

During one of my complaining episodes, Dr. Kleinschmidt sat by my bed and said, "Winifred, one month in a lifetime will scarcely be missed."

What a dear, wise man he was. And how correct. But I wanted to be up doing missionary work. I had come to realize that God was more interested in making me the servant He wanted me to be than in all the work I could do in my strength. Night after night as Dallas read to me from the Scripture, it seemed every verse had the word "wait" in it. "Wait on the Lord. Wait patiently for Him."

Finally Dr. Kleinschmidt decided I had a virus infection in either the muscle or central nervous system. He prescribed massive doses of penicillin to which I did not respond. Next he tried streptomycin to which I responded slowly.

We didn't know whether I would ever walk again until the Sunday before Thanksgiving. By then word of my illness had filtered back to the States and people were beginning to pray for us. I began to move my leg. As the numbers of our prayer intercessors grew, my recovery accelerated. By the Sunday after Thanksgiving—which we spent with the Kleinschmidts—I could walk a couple of steps.

Letter to Mom, November 1955:

Aba is a beautiful spot, located on two hills. One is hospital hill, the other station hill. It's warm here and the people are much more advanced. Even though it is just over the Sudanese border, the difference is incredible. What a contrast to our work in Sudan!

I have had a fresh gardenia, my wedding flower, at my bed almost every day. They are small, but what a delicious fragrance. And each day our cook picks oranges and grapefruit from the station trees for our meals. We have so much for which to be thankful.

CHAPTER 17

Back to the Work

We went home to Logotok in the beginning of December. On our return this time, we found suitcases of clothes, rock salt and food were among the many things stolen.

When we first returned, the weather was amazingly comfortable for the time of year. Then the hot weather settled in and the fires began. They looked so beautiful burning across the tops of the hills that it was hard to remember the danger they represented. Dallas worked hard to keep the areas around the station clear of grass and brush.

By mid-December I was able once more to do the housework though I was still limping. How wonderful to feel useful again.

The post office in Torit was still confused, but packages from home began to arrive with cake mixes and Jell-O that I had been out of for months. Christmas gifts also got through including a set of sister dresses for the girls and similar outfits for Kennie and Carlie. Kennie loved the rifle he received for Christmas though we had to have a talk with him when he frightened the Africans by pointing it at them. Many days the rifle was "out of reach" until Kennie became a better boy.

In early 1956 with the help of some of the African men, Dallas fired a kiln of 30,000 bricks. The bricks were made two at a time in a small, hand-operated compressor. Then they were placed on the ground to dry in the sun until stacked in the kiln. Each brick was placed in the kiln so the air could circulate around it.

For 24 hours a day from Monday to Friday, the kiln burned. Dallas supervised the men who kept the fires fresh and I provided coffee with sugar as an incentive to keep them all alert and awake.

Dallas wanted to use the bricks to build a church so there would be a permanent testimony in Logotok. Permission for this project was not given because government officials felt that better housing was more crucial. Still Dallas was able to build a pulpit from his bricks, and he hoped that some day a church would be built around it.

I told Mom she didn't need to send us peanut butter anymore. I was having it made by the Africans. They ground the peanuts between two stones and though we sometimes found stone chips in the finished product it was fine. The Latukas ate their peanuts raw but we convinced them they should roast ours before grinding them. They complied by roasting them in little piles of dried grass.

The Latukas ate mainly peanuts and grain. They ground the grain between two rocks, stirring the resultant flour into a pot of boiling water until it became a thick porridge. Then the men and boys ate first, dipping their hands into the pot. When they were finished, the women and girls ate.

After a year of displacement and illness, we were finally doing missionary work again. I started a women's class. Nine of the women sewed petticoats for themselves from the muslin Mom wrapped around our packages. They had never used needles before so it was a long process to get them to understand the concept of in-and-out stitches. They wore their finished petticoats under their abdomens instead of at their waists. That way the garments were useful whether they were pregnant or not.

I tried to teach the women Bible stories by using a flannelgraph but, because they weren't used to pictures, they didn't know how to interpret the figures. They couldn't understand that a flat picture of a tree represented the three dimensional, growing thing across the compound. We started with pictures from Nursery Department Sunday school materials.

In January we got the earthshaking news that Carolyn was accepted for first grade at Rethy Academy immediately. Mission officials decided that because of all the family illnesses and because of the debilitating climate of Sudan, she should begin school younger than usual.

"Oh, Dallas, not yet!"

"Honey, you knew she was going away to school," he said reasonably, though I knew he didn't want her to go any more than I did.

"But not until September. Not until she was seven and in second grade. She's only six years and four months!"

Barb and I spent a hectic three days sewing name tags into all her clothes and fretting about whether she had enough things to wear. Being the oldest, she had no hand-me-downs to swell her wardrobe and her clothes were also the ones that "walked" most frequently from the clothesline.

It was probably a good thing I didn't have much time to think about Carolyn's leaving. It was overwhelming enough as it was.

We took two days to drive to Rethy and we made certain we laughed a lot. When we arrived, we met Carolyn's two roommates, both in second grade. We put Carolyn's things away, hung up her clothes and encouraged her to keep her things neat. Then we left to find our own accommodations for the night.

We checked with her the next day. She had gotten herself up, made her bed, dressed herself and braided her hair. In fact she seemed to be doing much better than I was.

Carolyn liked school, except for the eating. It

was a rule that you had to drink your milk and eat a little of everything on your plate. The trouble was the powdered milk they served; she just had a hard time drinking it. Academically she did well, except for spelling. Somehow I had never gotten around to drilling her on that.

Back at Logotok once more, we experienced the *monyi-miji* dance in February. This celebration occurred once every 21 years when each generation of young men was inducted into the tribe as fathers of the village. Drums, drinking and dancing went on continuously for seven days. The men fought mock battles and "anointed" the heels of the young men with goat's blood mixed with manure. The large totem in the center of the village was made of old poles representing the older men and new poles were added for the new, young men. These poles were tied together in an upright position and were the center of the dance.

There were other occasions for dancing and the beating of the drums. When it was time to plant, there were big dances. Often the men covered their naked bodies with fine white ashes and looked like ghosts. There were hunting dances as well. The people sought to appease the "animal chief" by giving some of their cattle to him so he would give a good hunt. The Africans were excellent with their spears, but they liked it best when Bwana accompanied them with his gun.

These celebrations were hard on me because I had no help either at home or the hospital for their duration. Everyone was at the dance. Once I hired little boys of eight and nine to help but they took more of my time than the chores did.

Martha Hughell returned from her furlough and her language studies in Khartoum. She wanted to teach the local men Arabic and she began her boys' school with 20 boys.

For years the English had left education to the missionaries. Now, however, home rule placed education in the hands of the northern Arabs. Martha's school was closed by the authorities very quickly. Betty's girls' school was also closed. Only the medical work was allowed to continue unchecked. Often we wondered how long we would be allowed to remain in Sudan.

At the end of February, Carlie cut his first tooth and got his first haircut. Dallas tried to style his hair with the hand clippers, but the finished product looked like a stepladder. Carlie ended up with a buzz cut.

In mid-March he started walking, taking 15 steps on his first attempt. From that time on, there was no stopping him. He received his first pair of shoes, smiled sweetly at the lovely gift and promptly put them in his mouth. He had lots of nice outfits, but because of the heat, he wore only a diaper most of the time. He chatted constantly, saying nothing distinguishable.

I was back at a full medical schedule by now, though my leg still hurt and I still limped. I couldn't stoop or kneel and I had to push myself to do all that I felt I should do.

Dallas and I decided to leave Carlie with Barb and go on a safari with Kennie and Kay to the surrounding villages. We packed the Carry-All with cots, mosquito nets, table, chairs, Primus stove, lamps, food and other gear. We drove 300 miles from Monday to Thursday, taking the gospel to many places where it had never been heard. We had a wonderful time.

Dallas had purchased a loudspeaker with a record player that ran off the car battery.

"OK, Kennie. Turn it on," he'd say.

Kennie'd push the switch, music would pour out and the people would pour in. On previous trips we'd had trouble getting people to listen to us. They usually kept talking as we tried to sing or speak. But now they listened and marveled.

"It speaks Latuka," they would say, pointing at the loudspeaker.

Kay's white hair was a great fascination to the people, especially when we would visit a village that had never seen white people before. They would touch her head or try to pull out a hair and compare it to a hair from my head.

"How can a black-haired mother have a white-haired daughter?" they asked.

One night, just after we returned from the

safari, I went to the washroom and in my haste I didn't bother to light the kerosene lamp. I picked up the pitcher and poured the water over my hands into the metal basin. To my horror I poured a large, drowned rat onto my hands. Apparently it had climbed into the pitcher for a drink, been unable to get out and drowned. I shuddered for hours.

Carolyn came home in April at the conclusion of the first school term. She was rosy-cheeked and chubby from being in the cooler climate of Congo. When she got home, she slept for days adjusting to the hotter climate of Logotok.

Her teacher wrote, "She is one of the happiest little girls I have ever known." What a thrill to a mother's heart.

We were also thrilled by the development of Tomaso, a Latuka believer. He had been born Lohima, but after he trusted Christ, he took Tomaso as his name.

"I was one who doubted," he explained. "But like Thomas, I now believe."

Tomaso was our first convert to go off to Bible school. What a joy. We were concerned about the language barrier, but prayed he would learn to understand enough to study the whole Bible instead of just the few books in Latuka.

Tomaso and other young believers had gone to a large African conference in Congo and been amazed and encouraged by the hundreds of believers in attendance. They weren't alone in the world after all, something they hadn't previously understood. How narrow their worlds.

We were joined in our work at Logotok by Methusala, the African evangelist from Congo. What a help he was! The Africans had easily dismissed our religion as only for the white man, but when Methusala stood before them and preached, they couldn't duck the issue as easily.

Dallas also had the joy of returning to Opari for the ordination service of Pastor Anderaya. About 300 people gathered under a big tree as this outstanding African believer, already an evangelist for 20 years and a recent graduate of the Pastor's School in Congo, was ordained. Dallas got to preach the charge to the congregation.

But all our experiences weren't so positive.

May 1956, prayer letter:

Pray for our delinquent adherents! Some we thought had trusted Christ have gone back to the old traditional heathen practices. Our class of five believers is now down to two.

CHAPTER 18

Hard Medical Cases

One day after church, I went to the dispensary to give medicine. There under the tree was a young girl obviously in labor with her first baby. She had been in labor for 18 hours.

The Latukas never brought me maternity cases unless something was wrong.

"The baby is coming out back instead of front," said the old granny who was squatting in front of the crouching mother-to-be.

I checked the girl and the granny seemed to be right. I brought the girl inside the dispensary and 45 minutes later she was ready to deliver. There were signs of fetal distress, but a baby girl was finally born.

Several aunts, grandmas and cousins crowded into the room. All agreed the baby was dead.

"Not breathing."

Martha came to help and we worked over the baby for a long time. Finally we got her to breathe, though the village women still agreed she was dead. We took the baby up to Martha's house and put her on a hot water bottle.

The mother took the baby home to her village that night but she was back the next day. The baby wouldn't void or defecate.

Martha had tried giving the baby milk from a bottle the previous day, but the baby refused it. I tried sugar water from an eyedropper. She took some of it and after a while seemed better.

The women wanted me to name the baby, so I called her Kay. My Kay and Kennie decided the baby was Aunt Martha's since the baby had been in her house. After all, Aunt Martha didn't have a baby and should.

"When will Aunt Martha really get her own baby?" the kids asked.

The Africans asked the same thing of the single missionary women and even added, "Bwana Green, Bwana Senff and Bwana Doctor are there. Why can't they give you a baby?"

Our women delivered their babies either standing or squatting. They went through labor in the center of the village so everyone could see how brave they were. If they cried they believed the babies wouldn't come. If they lay down, the babies couldn't breathe. After delivery, the mother herself would dig a hole beside her hut and bury the placenta. When menstruation began again, she used absorbent leaves to catch the flow.

One of the babies I delivered when we were at Opari was named after Dallas. Dal-lees Greeen. The kids loved this cute little one and always wanted to hold him.

The saddest cases I saw were the babies, approximately seven days old, brought in by mothers saying they wouldn't nurse.

"Don't you have enough milk?" I'd ask the mother and she would respond by squirting a fine spray of milk from her breast.

Then I'd touch the baby's soft face and realize the problem. It had lockjaw and couldn't close its mouth to suckle. The cord had been cut with a dirty knife or rusty razor and infection had set in. There was nothing I could do; these babies would die in a short time.

One day four men carried a patient to the dispensary from 25 miles away. Their stretcher was an old canvas lawn chair.

"He is paralyzed," the bearers said. "And there is a hole."

There certainly was, in his head, about four inches in size, shaped like an X. The hole was full of cream-colored soft stuff I feared was brains exuding. I probed a bit with an instrument and was relieved to hit the hard skull. I cleaned out the goop, placed sterile packing in the hole and asked the family not to move the man.

The next morning he and his friends were nowhere to be found. I knew he would die if left in his village, so I sent Dallas out to bring him back. He eventually persuaded the group to get in the truck and come back for more care.

It distressed me to find my clean packing removed and the hole filled with the same mushy goop.

"What is this?" I asked.

No one would tell me.

"You must tell me," I insisted as I cleaned it out again. "I need to know if it has hurt him."

Eventually I pieced together that it was a fruit, chewed and spit into the opening. The fruit was not used for any purpose but medicine. I packed the wound with sterile dressings and again asked them to leave it alone. By this time the man was moving somewhat, so they followed my direction.

"What happened?" we asked. "How was he hurt?"

His father-in-law, we were told, had thrown a rock at him, connecting beyond his furthest expectations. Amazingly the man recovered. I don't know if his relationship with his father-in-law did.

Another day a man, with blood pouring from his mouth, came to see me. He had been chopping wood and a piece had flown up, hitting him in the chin, causing him to bite his tongue very badly. It was sliced right across the middle with a second jagged tear below that.

Not many things got to me but this did. I tried to suture it but the tongue was too tough for the needle to penetrate. Also, since there was no anesthetic, the man kept pulling away.

An inspiration hit. I had a few stainless steel skin clips. I inserted these at strategic places and they held until the healing began. I heard later that when the clips dropped out the man sold them for cash. His thanks to me was a sickly, half-dead chicken.

As I continued with my medical work averaging 80 to 100 patients a day and Dallas continued with his evangelism, we began making plans for that longed for occasion, our furlough. It was hard to believe we had been on the field for almost a full term.

In September we drove Carolyn back to Rethy for school, taking along her birthday presents and cards to be opened at the right time. The school would make a cake for her and make things as celebratory as possible.

We brought a live turkey back with us and cooked it to celebrate Kay's fourth birthday. It was quite a spectacle for the houseboys to see such a large bird butchered and cooked and eaten. Kay ordered a chocolate cake with pink icing which I happily and gratefully made.

I wrote to Mom who had invited us to stay with her during our furlough.

"Are you sure you know what you're doing?" I asked. "Your and Jackie's quiet, orderly lives will be turned upside down by my live wires.

"And I have a shock for you, Mom," I wrote.

"We're expecting number five at the end of February or the beginning of March. I feel like a heel with all the new clothes sent out for me to wear home but I'll bring them with me to wear later."

Since we were leaving to go home at the end of November, I wrote Mom asking that the kids not get too many presents for Christmas.

"Just being in the States will overwhelm them. They remember so little, if anything, about home."

Dallas and I talked often of how hard a transition the return would be for the children.

"They're used to acres of land to play on with only a few sheep or goats to shoo," Dallas said. "How will they handle neighbor's yards and cars?"

"And manners," I said. "We've tried to teach them good manners, but it's been so hard with what they see around them every day. We've been in the sticks too long."

I tried Carlie's snowsuit on him and Kay's coat on her. Once again we provided great amusement for our houseboys.

We left Logotok on Wednesday, November 21, 1956. The kids and I stayed in Katire while Dallas went to Rethy to pick up Carolyn.

On his way he counted 32 elephants, besides buffalo and other wild animals. When they were on their way back they had three flat tires and had to spend the night in the game reserve. Dallas and Carolyn slept in the truck and the the African boys slept under it. As usual there were the unexpected delays.

We spent Thanksgiving with our dear friends in Katire. Then we flew to Khartoum. Electricity, running water, two-story buildings, cars, noise, big stores, an ice cream parlor, street cars, planes and radios overwhelmed all of us and kept us from sleeping well.

Of course, our flight plans were changed because that was the nature of our whole African travel experience and because the Suez War had upset schedules dramatically. We were delighted that we were only one day late leaving Khartoum for Rome.

Rome! What congestion! What chaos! What insanity trying to sightsee with four kids and a five months' pregnant wife!

We next flew to Frankfurt, Germany, where we basked in the comforts Uncle Sam provides for the military. Friends bought Dallas a new coat and Kennie a heavy jacket with a fur collar. Because the short-lived Hungarian Revolution was underway, we donated our old coats to a clothing drive for Hungarian refugees.

The last leg of our trip took us through Gander, Newfoundland, for refueling. There we saw many Hungarian refugees in the waiting room. Our children played with some of their children, sharing the new toys they had been given in Germany. As we left, Kennie generously gave his newly acquired airplane to a Hungarian boy.

The night we crossed the Atlantic was one of the longest in my life. With four children crawling all over me outside and one kicking me inside, I was miserable. But how wonderful to finally see Mom and Jackie who had driven with Grandpa and my uncle to New York to meet us.

Of course, I cried and cried when we saw the family. Mom hugged me but had eyes only for the baby. She held Carlie for hours.

The cold weather was a wonder, especially to the kids. I spent my time trying to keep warm, tugging at my high school coat that I could only button at the neck because of my protruding stomach.

We went to Mom's hotel with her, and I will always remember the shock of hearing the black elevator operator speak English.

It was wonderful to be home!

Prayer letter, March 1957:

As we left the lazy, muddy Nile, infested with crocodiles, to wind its way around islands of "sud," we brought to a close our first term of missionary service. It has been a pioneer work in a very primitive section of southern Sudan, the youngest independent nation in Africa. One of Satan's last strongholds was invaded and he has done everything short of death to prevent the entrance of the gospel light into these darkened hearts.

We have seen the first Latuka translated from the

kingdom of darkness into the kingdom of God's dear Son. We have seen the first Acholi graduate from Bible school, prepared to evangelize his own people. We have seen the first Madi ordained to the gospel ministry.

Our hearts overflow with praise to the Lord for His protection through physical dangers, preservation through illness and provision in time of need.

Epilogue

We had a marvelous time celebrating Christmas 1956 at Mom's. Early in the new year, Dallas had a necessary operation, and on February 25, 1957, Larry Keith joined our family.

Prayer letter, September 1957:

We asked you to pray for Winifred's medical clearance. Now we are happy to report she has a chance to be relieved of her back pain. God has graciously led us to a Christian neurosurgeon who gave a thorough examination and a definite diagnosis. She is scheduled to enter Methodist Hospital in Philadelphia for a laminectomy September 23. We covet your continued prayer for her, that she will have a speedy and complete recovery so our return to the field will not be unduly delayed. The operation requires about three months recuperation, so we will look forward to going back to Sudan sometime in the spring.

Prayer letter, February 1958:

We trust you will rejoice with us at this time (Psalm 126:3). The Lord has done great things for us and we are exceedingly glad. In January we visited Winifred's surgeon, and he said she may return to the field after April 1. Other physical problems of the family have, one by one, been cleared up so that we are ready to return to the field.

Prayer letter, May 30, 1958:

"O the depth of the riches both of the wisdom and knowledge of God! how unsearchable are His judgments, and his ways past finding out! For who hath known the mind of the Lord? or who hath been his counselor? Or who hath first given to him, and it shall be recompensed unto him again? For of him, and through him, and to him, are all things: to whom be glory for ever. Amen" (Romans 11:33-36).

SURPRISE may be your reaction to this letter. It is different from anything we ever anticipated writing. Since we last wrote, we have been busy packing, getting shots and participating in farewell meetings. In spite of all this, instead of cruising through the blue Mediterranean enroute to Africa, we are still living out of our suitcases at Winifred's mother's home.

Instead of planning for another term of work in the Sudan, we are now trying to line up a job of service here in the States for the immediate future. How did all this come about?

SHOCKING is the word. When we returned from a series of farewell meetings, we found notification from the mission of the cancellation of our bookings to Africa for medical reasons. Consultation with the field doctor had confirmed that Kennie, who suffered seriously from cerebral malaria last term, should be protected from repeated attacks.

Now he is under special treatment for three or four years. Hopefully, after this time, there will be no more danger to him. Pray this may be so!

Winifred is steadily improving but has a long way to go before her strength is restored. Since there is so much doubt about the health of two members of our family, the mission has put us on "extended furlough."

A great missionary statesman reminded us, "You have to accept this as the Lord's will for your lives at this time."

A longtime friend said, "Sometimes what looks like a tangent proves to be the main part of God's plan."

We ask you to pray with us for a place to live as well as a job. We want to be where we can be useful in His service. We are resting on Romans 8:28 and our motto is, "His 'will is our peace' "

SUSPENSE was ended as God answered these prayers of our supporters, and Dallas became the first pastor of Southwood Baptist Church in Woodbury, New Jersey, where he served for two years. Then God led us back into missions when he became Deputation Secretary for North African Mission, now Arab World Mission. Later he joined the staff of

BCM International, formerly Bible Club Movement, where he served until his "retirement" in 1992. At the time of writing, he is enjoying a modified ministry at Calvary Fellowship Church, Downingtown, PA as minister of missions and mercy.

Carolyn is married to Tom Fink, professor at Philadelphia College of Bible, and is the mother of three nearly grown children.

Ken and his wife, Belkis, live in Indiana where Ken manages a country club.

Kay, married to Jerome Iverson and the mother of two, lives in Crystal Lake, IL where Jerome is a Christian clinical psychologist.

Carl lives with his wife, Patsy, and their three daughters and serves as pastor of Calvary Fellowship Church, Downingtown, PA.

Larry is headmaster at Plumstead Christian School, Plumstead, PA, and is married to Jane.

As for me, my back defined my life for several years. I had several back surgeries in 1957 and 1959. From 1968 until 1970, I was confined to bed with back problems, and in 1969 I had a spinal fusion.

In the years before I became bedridden, I became involved with Bible clubs.

One day Bessie Traber founder of the Bible Club Movement asked me if I'd be willing to teach a childrens' Bible club.

I shook my head. "I've never taught kids," I said.

"You have five of your own," Miss Traber said.

"Are you telling me you don't teach them?"

So I began a Bible club, then another and another. Eventually I oversaw 16 clubs and taught three or four.

It was during the two years I was in bed that God opened another door for an unexpected and wonderful ministry for me. Often women who came to visit me would tell me about their marriage problems. I became convinced that many of the problems were solvable by application of the biblical principles concerning marriage.

After my spinal fusion and the long period of recuperation and time for study, I was invited to teach the program I developed as a result of the talks with those women. "Living with Love" has now been taught all over the United States and in many places around the world as I've traveled abroad each year. Audio and video tapes have also gone to places where I've not been. God has opened a Bible teaching ministry for me to women here and abroad. I can only praise God for the results I've seen as lives have been changed as they've sought God's way through their difficulties and problems.

As for Sudan, two words describe this country from 1954 to the present: WAR and FAMINE.

Tens of thousands have died of starvation, a situation greatly amplified by the civil war-created refugee problems. Those who live in towns often cannot step outside the town limits due to martial law, and those in the bush are unable to move to areas better able to support them because many roads are mined and booby trapped. The hills have been denuded of their sparse brush and trees, and people have neither places nor knowledge to grow gardens in the severe weather. One Christian man of our acquaintance has not seen his family in seven years.

In spite of atrocities, hunger, deprivation and isolation, the church has continued to grow. In August 1992, we heard there were approximately 250,000 Christians in 260 churches ranging in size from 50 to 600 believers.

As Pastor Anderaya said, "If it were your church or my church, it would die. But it is the Lord's church, and it will not die."